Five Steps to Freedom

Five Steps to Freedom

An Introduction to Spiritual Mind Treatment

John B. Waterhouse, Ph.D.

Foreword by Marilyn Leo, D.D.

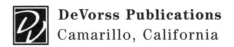

DeVorss Publications
Camarillo, California

Five Steps to Freedom
Copyright© 2003 by John B. Waterhouse.

ISBN: 978-087516-842-5
Fourth Printing, 2024

Notice: The purpose of this book is to educate. It is sold with the understanding that the publisher and author shall have neither liability nor responsibility for any injury or alleged injury to be caused directly or indirectly by the information contained in this book. Each person's health, spiritual, emotional, mental, and creative needs are unique. To obtain recommendations appropriate to your particular situation, please consult a qualified competent professional.

DeVorss & Company, Publisher
P.O. Box 1389
Camarillo CA 93011-1389
www.devorss.com

Printed in the United States of America

CONTENTS

ACKNOWLEDGEMENTS

It is the students of Science of Mind principles throughout the world that I must first acknowledge. It is because of their enthusiasm and hunger for Truth Principles that I am called to share these teachings more widely.

I am grateful to the many members and friends of the Center for Creative Living, and especially to those class members who helped me develop my ideas with their many excellent questions and voracious appetite for a deeper understanding of these teachings.

My editors and proofreaders Marilyn Leo, D.D., Leslie Petrovich, and Robert Waldrup, Ph.D. have been enormously supportive throughout the development of this project.

And most important of all, I must thank my beloved wife and co-minister, Barbara Waterhouse for her constant encouragement and deep insights into the nuances of practicing Spiritual Mind Treatment.

FOREWORD

Unless we change our thoughts, words and intentions today, our tomorrows will repeat our yesterdays. *Five Steps To Freedom* will give you tools to make those changes. However, this endeavor must be a conscious one, done with patience and practice. But believe me, in the words of Ernest Holmes, you can change your life by changing your thinking.

Ernest Holmes created a philosophy of thought that was much in alignment with Ralph Waldo Emerson, Judge Thomas Troward, Jesus of Nazareth, and others. He brought together a compilation of the thinking of great minds throughout the ages and called it Science of Mind. According to Reginald Armor in *That Was Ernest,* [Ernest Holmes] "[He] had the immovable conviction that he never walked alone; that there is 'a light that lighteth every man that cometh into this world.' He sought always to walk in this light and depend on it for guidance. Dr. Holmes sensed God everywhere and felt that the guidance of Spirit was a very real experience."

Early on he discovered that when certain principles are used for good, there are predictable, repeated outcomes or demonstrations. He, along with his brother Fenwicke Holmes, opened a sanitarium in 1917 for people who desired Ernest Holmes' treatment, which was an affirmative type of prayer. Ernest Holmes called this prayer *mind treatment* because treatment was the term used by doctors, and he declared that the affirmative prayer he used was scientific in nature and would produce healing results when used. Therefore, it filled the role of treatment. Though Holmes never wanted to give a formula for spiritual mind treatment, in his book *The Science of Mind,* he sets forth three steps in the chapter titled "The Practice of Science of Mind Healing," which he believes are effective in coming to a place of "knowing" the Truth: wholeness.

Many years later, Orin Moen, then head of the Education Department of the Institute of Religious Science, believed it to be helpful to create a guideline for treatment and added the steps of Thanksgiving and Release. At other times in our history, additional people created four steps, six steps, and I've heard that there can be as many as sixteen. This book, however, is setting forth/proposing five steps. The author is thorough in his explanation and guidance of the five steps and provides work pages for your practice in writing the steps of treatment. However, we must remember that a change in our awareness of who we are and our relationship *in* Divine Spirit is what will bring about changes in our lives. "The realization of the Presence of God is the most powerful healing agent known . . ." *Science of Mind,* page 145. This means in all situations.

We now refer to this healing tool as Spiritual Mind Treatment because that is what it is. We treat our minds to be in alignment with Spirit or Divine Mind. We consciously use the Divine Spirit to embrace the Allness of Life, to release doubts or fears and to come to a full realization of God or Spirit *as* our lives. I keep saying "or" because it does not really matter what you call It.

The words must be from your heart, the depth of your being.

People often ask if they have to say the words of treatment in lovely, flowery words that are not like the way they speak. I respond by asking, "How can you be authentic and feel deeply about your relationship in Spirit if the words are not your own?" If you have what some may call a "gruff" personality, sweet words and phrases are going to be meaningless to you, to your psyche, to your consciousness. Your words in treatment must be just that, *your* words—words that have meaning to you, not to someone else. I am reminded of the youngster who was asked to give the blessing at the dinner table and his words were, "Yea God, thanks for the grub!" Jesus' words were very simple when he healed people. There was always a phrase of gratitude and the feeling behind his words "Take up thy bed and walk" had great strength and faith. When he spoke his word, there was nothing that stood in the way of the healing. And in Truth, there is nothing to stand in the way of our own words and healing, other than our own doubts and fears.

I personally do not ask God to heal me when I am sick. I know that the Truth of me is Spirit and Spirit is never sick. It knows nothing unlike its own perfection. But I must *know* this, and what I must do is talk to myself until I am convinced of this Truth. When I am convinced and *know* this Truth, I am well and healed.

It is now time to step forward and practice this magnificent technique for healing.

—*Rev. Dr. Marilyn Leo*

PREFACE

Why Freedom?

Freedom is among the most powerful and predominate ideas expressed in American culture. As Americans we insist on having the freedom to acquire, to accomplish, and to believe whatever we choose. Yet with the promise of freedom that is as old as America herself, we continue to find ourselves bound to ideas that hold us back from experiencing our lives as fully and richly as we would like.

Five Steps to Freedom is about freeing ourselves from these limiting thoughts and beliefs that have kept us from living the lives we so deeply desire. This book is about freeing ourselves to create joy, happiness, prosperity, vibrant health, meaningful work, and fulfilling relationships in our lives. This is the freedom that satisfies our thirst for significance and contentment.

This book is about freeing ourselves from hoping that God or some other perceived force or authority would have the power to bestow upon us a more meaningful existence. This is the freedom to know without question or reservation that we control our own destinies in every moment of every day of our lives.

This book is about freeing ourselves from trying, because when we try, our thoughts can sound like, "If I would just work harder at being spiritual by saying more prayers or by meditating more often or by being more spiritual, then my internal doubts, fears, confusion, or pain would go away." This is the freedom to know that we already have a spiritual legacy and that all we need to do is claim that legacy, and it is ours.

This book is about freeing ourselves from any sense of failure that would have us believe we are off course with our lives and that somehow we've made terrible mistakes that will keep us from achieving our dreams. This is the freedom of knowing how beautifully, how wonderfully, and how amazingly our lives are unfolding today and every day.

By reading this book and completing the exercises in it, you will discover a powerful new way of relating to all of life. You may even develop a new awareness of yourself that will expand the possibilities of your life in extraordinary and profound ways. As you stand on this threshold of a new sense of freedom, I welcome your clear attention and focus. And as much as this is a journey of thoughts and ideas, it is equally a journey of the heart. So, I invite you to open yourself to this dance of life and allow your soul to sing the brilliant song of Spirit in all you think, feel, say and do.

Many years ago I discovered within myself an idea that perfectly describes the meaning and purpose of my life. The words I use to describe this idea are these:

> *My purpose is to reveal and release the power of the human spirit, wherever I am and in whatever I do."*

My intention in sharing the ideas of *Five Steps to Freedom* is to do exactly that. When the power within us is revealed and released, we are absolutely free to live our lives to the fullest potential. When we are consciously aware of the power we wield, we are free to live in our wholeness, expressing and experiencing the Divine Love that we are.

Preface: Why Freedom?

As we begin this journey, I offer you a short and simple affirmation that expresses the essence of freedom I seek to reveal. These words help me to remember what is truly meaningful in life. I invite you to read it several times and allow it to move through you, touching that deep place within that knows this is the Truth:

I live in a world created by Love,
Love is what I am.
In all the I think and say and do,
Love is what I am.
Before me, behind me, around me, inside me,
Love is what I am.
I'm filled overflowing and clear in my knowing,
Love is what I am.

Redefining Prayer

This book explores the use of prayer in our daily lives.

The idea of using prayer as the means by which one speaks to God is ancient in its origins. Getting down on one's knees and praying to a deity for comfort or support has been a human discipline for thousands of years. This tradition has little to do with what I will be sharing with you. The form of prayer described and outlined in this book may seem very different from what we were taught as children and what many of us have used as prayer throughout our lives.

You are about to learn a new way of praying that will call you to look at all of life with new eyes and to experience the presence of God from an entirely new perspective. This new form of prayer, known as Spiritual Mind Treatment, may require that you establish a fundamentally new relationship with the Divine, and equally important perhaps, create an entirely new understanding of who you are within that relationship.

As human beings, we use many different methods of expression. We speak, sing, write, dance, build, work, play, and so on. We use our bodies and minds to express ourselves and to feel connected to life.

Yet, our culture and many other world cultures hold prayer as being a more mystical and spiritual activity than any of these methods of expression. Is this true? Are we more holy or more closely connected to God when we pray? Are the words we use when we pray more sacred than those we use in conversation with one another?

To explore the meaning of prayer, I offer the following questions for your consideration:

When Do We Pray?

Some say they pray only when they go to church. Others say they pray only when they find themselves in trouble or without an answer in dangerous or deeply important situations. Some say they set aside a special time to pray each day without regard to what is going on, and many say they never pray at all.

According to the understanding I wish to share with you, all of these answers and most others fall short of explaining the true essence of prayer. To answer the question of *"when,"* we will need more information about the *"what"* of prayer.

What Is Prayer?

Probably the simplest and most common answer is that prayer is talking to God. If this is so, then we must ask, "What does it mean to talk to God?" This question then brings us to a litany of related questions, such as:

- When we pray, how do we know we are being heard?
- Are our needs tended to only when we pray for assistance?
- Are our prayers always considered and responded to?
- When we pray, should we use specific words and phrases?
- Is it important to be respectful when we pray?
- Do these or any particular conditions help make our prayers more effective?

Answers to these questions will be as varied as the people who provide them. They all speak to our differing perceptions of God, but none of these answers or questions move us toward understanding the true meaning of prayer. So, we go back to the basic question, "What is prayer?" For the purpose of this exploration, I will define prayer as "any expression directed toward God." This could also be stated as "any expression received by God."

Virtually every religion and spiritual discipline teaches that the Divine is always present in our lives. If this is true, then God, or Spirit must be aware of every word we speak or write, every idea we imagine, and every action we take. Spirit is aware of everything we express because it is impossible for us to express outside of this Divine Presence. This leads us to the logical conclusion that everything we express in our lives is prayer.

In response you might say that this cannot be so because we are not always addressing God in our daily activities. The problem with this argument is that God is not an observer in our lives; God is the consciousness of our lives. We will explore this idea more deeply in the next chapter.

As we begin to more fully comprehend the constant and abiding presence of Divine Spirit, we will find ourselves entertaining the notion that our every utterance, our every thought and absolutely everything we express into life is a calling out to God. Every time we curse, we are praying. Every time we are angry, we are praying. Every time someone tells a joke, or laughs, or lies, or cries, what is happening is prayer. Our judgments are prayers. Our fears and phobias are prayers. Spirit is present in the midst of it all. Everything we think, say and do is a prayer, and every bit of it is having a direct and significant effect on our lives.

But most often we don't even remember what we say, much less what thoughts run through our minds. How could these fleeting impressions be so important? Please understand that our thoughts, no matter how fleeting or seemingly unimportant they may appear, are vitally important in how we experience life. Thoughts are the building blocks of all human experience. Our personal realities are based upon what we, as individuals believe. Our beliefs control our lives and even the most fleeting thoughts make an impression on our sense of what is real and what is not.

How Our Beliefs Filter Our Experiences

As human beings we are constantly processing massive amounts of information. When we believe something is so, we will accept only information that supports our belief until we are willing to change that belief. Having beliefs is an innate characteristic of the human psyche, and our entire understanding of life is based on the sum total of what we have believed to be so from our very earliest memories to right now. Until we are willing to change what we believe, our minds will tend to reject anything that is contrary to our individual beliefs.

As an example of how this works, I offer the following story:

I was recently flying back from a conference in Colorado to my home in North Carolina. It was winter and the last weather report I had heard before leaving Colorado was that most of North Carolina had experienced a blanketing of snow the day before. As we were landing, it was early evening and I commented to the man sitting next to me that I could see snow on the ground along the runway.

In response he said, "There is no snow."

Again I looked out the window and as we were taxiing toward the terminal, the flashing lights on our plane were revealing clearly to me that the ground beyond the runway was covered with snow.

I immediately responded, "No, that's snow."

He again retorted, "There is no snow."

But I was seeing snow and I'd heard that weather report and just knew what I was seeing had to be snow. My neighbor then explained that he had spoken with his wife just before our plane departed, and she had shared that it had been a warmer than expected day and all the snow had quickly melted. There was no snow.

Now I'm a fairly intelligent guy with good eyesight. Yet, because I accepted the information I had received in Colorado as accurate, I allowed myself to believe something that was not so. In reflection, I realize that there is another element to this story. I grew up in South Florida and have lived in the South and Southwestern parts of the United States all my life. Snow is still a rare experience in my life, and I have a childish intrigue with its presence. There was a part of me that wanted snow on the ground as I arrived home to North Carolina. I wanted and anticipated snow on the ground that evening, so that is what I experienced. Once I was willing to consider new information, although disappointed, I was willing to shift my reality and see that there was no snow.

This is a simplified example of how our beliefs filter our experiences. Our reality is influenced by our beliefs. Anyone who has not experienced this is likely far too attached to his or her beliefs and has become inflexible to higher levels of understanding.

So, what does this have to do with prayer? My point is that our beliefs dictate how prayer works for us. If we believe that a certain way of praying works better than another, then it does. If we believe that certain elements must be present for our prayers to be effective, then those elements must be present.

Living Our Prayer

The way we live our lives *is* our prayer. Our beliefs and perceptions drive our lives. If there is something, anything that we want to change about our lives, the change comes through our prayer, meaning changes come in response to how we live our lives and what we believe about ourselves and about our world.

Below I revisit the questions asked earlier in this chapter, in light of our new understanding of prayer:

Q. When we pray, how do we know we are being heard?

A. Our prayers are so much more than simply heard. All our thoughts and spoken words exist within the Mind of God, therefore, all thoughts are creations of God as much as they are creations of the one who thinks them.

Q. Are our needs tended to only when we pray for assistance?

A. Our thoughts, spoken words and actions are our prayers. Our lives exist within a perfect balance, which means that we are not given what we need, or even what we want. Rather, our lives are a perfect reflection of who we are.

Q. Are our prayers always considered and responded to?

A. Again, Life reflects back to us that which dwells within our thoughts and beliefs.

Q. When we pray, should we use specific words and phrases?

A. Praying is not so much about language as it is about the way we express into the world with our beliefs, emotions, and attitudes. Using specific phrases has value only in as much as it helps us keep our minds clear and focused on the life we choose to experience.

Q. Is it important to be respectful to God when we pray?
A. Respect is not a condition of prayer. God is equally present in the mundane and the magnificent aspects of life.

Q. Do these or any particular conditions help make our prayers more effective?
A. Our prayers are the sum total of everything we think, say and do. Therefore, the more consciously aware we are of our own thoughts, words, and actions, the more effective our lives become.

Whether these answers seem clear or confusing, I encourage you to keep reading. As we learn more about the meaning and practice of the five-step process of Spiritual Mind Treatment, we will be simultaneously developing a powerful new understanding of how Spirit works and how we can fully engage this Divine Presence in the daily experience of our individual lives.

Spiritual Mind Treatment

If there is something in your life or mine that we seek to change, there are methods for creating powerful changes no matter how difficult or hopeless the conditions before us may seem. By changing the way we think, speak and act, our prayers become more effective. And as our prayers become more effective, we can literally see our world changing around us.

The key to these changes dwells in how well we know Spirit and how well we know ourselves in relation to Spirit. The most effective way I have learned to do this is through the practice of Spiritual Mind Treatment and through understanding the spiritual principles on which this practice is based.

Spiritual Mind Treatment is about each of us becoming intimately involved in the creation of our own lives. It's about claiming the life we desire and being the masters of our own destiny. Spiritual Mind Treatment is "Power Praying." Its purpose is to be a tool that helps us focus our attention and create intention in our lives with extraordinary energy and clarity.

Spiritual Mind Treatment consists of a five-step mental and spiritual process in which each step brings an ingredient essential to the whole. Each of the next five chapters is dedicated to one of these steps. At the end of each chapter, you are given space to practice and develop your own personal expression of that step.

I encourage you to do these exercises as they present themselves. If you do not want to write in your book, do your work on separate paper, but please do the exercises. Without doing the exercises, this book can be no more to you than an "interesting read." Writing your own Spiritual Mind Treatments will allow you to internalize the methods shared in a much more meaningful and personal way.

Spiritual Mind Treatment is a method of expressing ourselves in ways that open us up to experiencing the fullest possible understanding of our world and ourselves. Enjoy this adventure. It holds a key to some of the deepest and most profound revelations that life has to offer.

Ernest Holmes on Prayer...

Prayer is nothing but a mental attitude. Prayer is nothing you eat, nothing you smell, nothing you taste, nothing your feel, but you cannot pray without thinking. Every word is an audible expression of a thought, and therefore, the ultimate essence of prayer is your thought. . . . It is nothing but a simple and direct, positive believing, a mental attitude. That is all that prayer is.

Love and Law (2001), p. 127.3

If prayer has been answered, it is not because God has been moved to answer one man and not another, but because one man more than another has moved himself into a right relationship with the Spirit or the Principle of Being – whichever one chooses to call It.

The Science of Mind (1938), p. 281.1

In the Science of Mind, which is a conscious use of the creative energy of the Law of Life, mental treatment is the art, the act, and the science of using this Law for the purpose of producing a definite, objective, manifest result.

This Thing Called Life (1943), p. 46.3

STEP ONE

Recognition

Recognizing the Presence of Spirit

*God is a circle whose centre is everywhere
and whose circumference is nowhere.*

—VOLTAIRE

The teachings of Science of Mind are based wholly on the premise that "God is all there is." This means that God creates all things and contains all of creation within Itself, which is to say that all of creation consists of "God-stuff." If this is a new or unexplored concept for you, I invite you to resist taking a position for or against it too quickly. Instead, simply consider the possibility that this idea is worth exploring through the reading of the next few pages. If like most people, you grew up being told that God was someone in a place called Heaven, this chapter offers you an opportunity to reframe your perceptions in a way that will broaden and deepen your understanding of the Divine.

When we hold onto a belief or perception for most of our lives, it can be challenging to embrace a concept that appears so radically different from what we have grown comfortable in believing. This is especially so when we have used a viewpoint to repeatedly define important aspects of our lives. If we have held God as someone to whom we can turn or from whom we can ask for help, redefining that perception will require a major shift in

11

consciousness. Understanding Spirit as the sum total of "all that is" may be a challenging concept to embrace, but there are some great advantages to experiencing Spirit within this new paradigm.

I invite you to remain open to the possibility of God being bigger than you have ever imagined. By seeing Spirit in this new way, we expand our perception of life itself.

What If This Was Your Job?

Imagine for a moment that you are the creator of the universe back at the beginning of time. How would you go about creating? You certainly could create something outside of yourself, which you would then be able to observe. Having an observable creation, you could interact with it and manipulate it; you could be pleased with it or displeased with it; you could preserve it or you could destroy it. This perception of the creative process is easy to understand and accept because it reflects upon our own human nature. It is how many people believe life and physical form has come to exist, yet it is based on a very limited, anthropomorphic perception of God that falls far short of recognizing the true essence of the Divine.

The Spanish philosopher Benedict de Spinoza once said that if a triangle could describe God, it would describe God as a triangle. This idea suggests that we as human beings tend to limit the parameters of our spiritual understanding to our limited understanding of ourselves. The Bible says that man was created in the image and likeness of God. However, humans have created a perception of God that mirrors the image and likeness of how we perceive ourselves. This primitive and very narrow way of perceiving Spirit no more accurately represents our creation than those presented in Greek, Roman or Nordic mythologies.

Now, consider the idea that you are pure consciousness and have within you the unlimited potential to create in whatever way you choose. Wouldn't you choose to create in such a way that every expression was yours to express and every experience was yours to experience? Haven't you ever wanted to be a bird or a cloud or a dolphin or some other expression of life so you could experience just how glorious that life form must be?

Consider how much more natural and reasonable this feels in relating to the creation of all life. A universe created within Spirit would be a universe in which everything had intelligence and in which everything experienced and expressed the Divine by means of its very existence. This is what Spirit does. Spirit expresses through the creative process, and Spirit experiences that which is expressed. Everything exists within this flow of information through which matter and energy animate the entire universe into this dance of expressing and experiencing life.

Understanding the Essence of Spirit

Understanding that Spirit is all there is, is not a destination—it's a direction. I know of no one who can legitimately claim to fully comprehend the Divine, even though many claim to do so. It is inconceivable that the human mind could even approach fully knowing every aspect of the infinite smallness and infinite largeness of Spirit. How could anyone fully understand the limitless potential of that which transcends all dimensions, all time and all space? I do not believe it is possible. However, there are three defining concepts that will help in developing a clearer understanding of Spirit. These three aspects of perceiving the boundlessness of Spirit are known as Omnipresence, Omniscience, and Omnipotence. Each has been used in theological discourse for generations, yet for the purpose of this exploration, we will be expanding our understanding of the truth that dwells within them. Even with the limitations of language, these three ideas may offer us a way to begin wrapping our minds around the "infinite allness" of Spirit.

Spirit is Omnipresent

Spirit is present everywhere. Traditionally this idea was used theologically to suggest that God was always available to us; that if we called out, God would hear; if we needed God's assistance, God would always be there. The intended result was either to be comforted by knowing that God was always wherever we were, or to be perpetually on one's best behavior because God was always there watching. Yet, the concept of omnipresence offers us so much more, not only in understanding the infinite presence of Spirit, but all of life.

Omnipresence means that nothing in physical form or otherwise exists outside the presence of Spirit. Everything that your five senses can perceive, whether visible or invisible; whether you can hold it in your hand or see it only through a microscope or a telescope; whether you can hear it, smell it, taste it or touch it; It is all Spirit. Whether you are aware of something's presence or completely oblivious to it, if it exists, then it is Spirit. Every thought by you or anyone else, every image you ever imagined and every idea that has not yet taken form in your mind already exists fully within the Mind of Spirit.

All creation exists within Spirit; nothing exists outside of Spirit because there is no outside. Everything including the smallest and most fundamental quantum levels of physical form, every thought, every action and everything that has the potential to exist, exists within the Oneness of Spirit. Spirit is energy, Spirit is light, Spirit is darkness, Spirit is form, Spirit is formless; whatever is, must be Spirit. There is nothing outside of Spirit because Spirit is boundless and limitless. Spirit is omnipresent because everything and everywhere is Spirit.

Spirit is Omniscient

Spirit is all knowing. Traditionally this concept was used to explain how God knew all our thoughts and everything we said and did, which was interpreted to mean that all our sins and transgressions would forever be on record in heaven. This gave way to the need for someone to intercede on our behalf and arrange for us a form of divine forgiveness. This idea ranges as far from helping us to understand the true essence of Spirit as I can imagine.

The all-knowingness of Spirit demonstrates that all knowledge and intelligence dwells within the mind of Spirit. It means that Spirit is every thought, every dream, every idea, every emotion, every vision, all natural and spiritual law and every other expression of consciousness that has ever and could ever exist.

If Spirit is all there is, then our thoughts and our words are the thoughts and words of Spirit. They are expressed by Spirit, move through Spirit, and are received and experienced by Spirit.

Your mind and my mind are not separate minds. Everything we experience exists in the Mind of Spirit. No thought is ever lost and nothing experienced will ever be forgotten because of the awesome information collection system called Universal Mind.

Hypnotists regress people to help them recall specific details of past events, which they have been unable to remember. Under hypnosis, many individuals suddenly remember even the minutest details of past circumstances with stunning accuracy. This exemplifies the constant accessibility of all information past, present, and future.

Psychic activity is collected in a similar yet expanded way. Psychics are more open and attuned to information held in Universal Mind. We all have moments when we know something has or is about to happen without having ever been told by anyone. All of these are examples of how Universal Mind, the Mind of Spirit, continues to be the inexhaustible and infinite collection point of all of life's experiences.

Spirit is omniscient, all knowing, because as Creator of all that is, there is nothing that is separate from Spirit including all knowledge, all information and all understanding.

Spirit is Omnipotent

Spirit is all-powerful. In traditional theology, this concept is used to suggest that God has the power to direct, manipulate and intercede in our lives. If we believe that God's omnipotence is a power over all life, especially the lives of all human beings, then we are likely to conclude that we must know and abide by God's will so as to avoid the wrath or rebuke of this all-powerful deity. God having power over anything creates a duality of wills that guarantees perpetual conflict between God and people. What results is the idea that we are destined to fall short of God's expectations and are subject to God's eternal domination. *Let that idea go!* The omnipotence of Spirit is not a challenge or limitation to our lives; rather, it is a unifying principle that demonstrates the magnificence of all life.

The omnipotence of Spirit means that everything that is power is Spirit. Spirit is the cosmic glue that forms galaxies into patterns of magnificent color and design. Spirit powers the emission of unfathomable amounts of light and energy from every star in the universe. Spirit is the power that holds the planets in orbit around the sun. Spirit is the power of earthquakes, hurricanes, tides and ocean currents. The gravitational force that holds us to the surface of the earth is the power of Spirit. All the energy that powers worldwide telecommunications, every form of transportation, all the appliances in your home, the energy to print this book all are the power of Spirit. Spirit is the power of all movement, all energy regardless how massively cosmic or how small and insignificant the demonstration of that power may be.

That which powers our very existence is Spirit. The power behind every system in our bodies, the beating of our hearts, the filling and emptying of our lungs, the firing synapses in our brains are all Spirit. All forms of personal power—physical, mental, emotional, psychic or otherwise—are Spirit. If it is power, then it is Spirit.

Raise your arm up into the air. Go ahead raise it! The power it took to do that is Spirit. Spirit is the power of every idea, every intention and every desire you and I have ever imagined. Spirit *is* the greatest power in the universe.

The power of the Divine is absolute and unchallenged. Spirit is Omnipotent, all-powerful because there is no power outside of Spirit.

By aligning these three concepts, we can begin to understand the limitlessness of Spirit in our lives and throughout all creation. Spirit is present in stone, and in water, and in fire because these things could not exist without the presence, power and intelligence of Spirit within them. And seeing the presence of Spirit, feeling the power of Spirit, and knowing the intelligence of Spirit in everything calls us to a higher state of consciousness and into a more intimate connection with all of life.

Spirit as a Unity

Another way we can more fully recognize the wholeness of Spirit is to observe Spirit as a unity. This means that even though Spirit may have distinguishable elements, Spirit cannot be divided into parts. Being a unity, Spirit is the single and exclusive source of power in the universe. If there were two sources of power, there would be conflict in every point of the space-time continuum, and chaos would prevail everywhere and always. This is not happening. We live in a world where peace and harmony are the natural state of being. Expressions of aggression and disharmony do exist but represent unnatural states that inevitably, and often quickly, burn themselves out.

Being a unity, Spirit is absolute in every possible way, in every dimension, in every mathematical calculation, in every form and every potential. The oneness of Spirit prevails without exception, from the grandest universal scale to the tiniest probability of matter. Everything exists within this indivisible oneness of Spirit.

Experiencing the Oneness of Spirit

Scientists have been telling us for some time now that we live in the world of illusion, meaning that our senses do not reveal the highest reality of the world we observe. Physicists know that there are no hard edges to anything that has physical form. As soon as we step into a room, we are immediately exchanging particles with every other organic and inorganic form in that room. By breathing out, we are releasing particles that have been part of every organ system in our bodies. By breathing in, we are receiving airborne particles into our bodies, not only from other humans, but also from plants, insects, microbes, and even from inanimate materials that are all around us. Our sense of smell is simply a tool we use to detect particles of matter in significant enough numbers so as to register an olfactory response in our brains. Most of the particles we breathe in are not in significant enough numbers to register any awareness of smell, but we are, nonetheless taking them in. And it doesn't stop there.

Each one of us has an energy field (also called an aura) that extends out beyond the edges of our visible bodies. We know it exists because it has been measured through the process of Kirlian photography. This energy field is the container of your emotional body. It becomes larger or smaller in size depending upon how we are relating to our environment. When we greet someone or enter a space that feels comfortable and welcoming, our energy fields expand. This means that when we are in a room together or physically close to one another, we are not just standing or sitting near one another, we are actually intermingling our energies within one another's emotional bodies. Talk about being cozy!

The world revealed to us through our senses is only a limited part of what is going on. There is much more happening all around us than we are able to consciously comprehend. When we limit ourselves to our sensory awareness, we miss most of life. However, if we choose to embrace the idea that Spirit is all there is, fully present everywhere in and as all things, then we can begin to open ourselves to the allness of Spirit. With this recognition, our perceptions change, and our world begins to appear very differently.

Neutralizing Judgment

As we begin to embrace the notion that all things exist within the Oneness of Spirit, we realize that our crotchety neighbor is a perfect out-picturing of that same Spirit. The same is true for that boss, teacher, or acquaintance we never liked. Ultimately, we realize that every driver on the road exists within this same Divine Oneness, as does every person who has ever annoyed us in line at the bank or the grocery store, and so on throughout all our relations.

All human beings constantly express with Divine authority, whether their expressions exist only in the recesses of their minds or are being broadcast to every corner of the world, whether their experiences call them to laugh or to cry, whether their ideas are expansive or reflective, whether they know who they are or have no conscious awareness of the power they wield. Whatever is expressed is an expression of Spirit.

In the same way that we all express the Divine, we also experience in return the full and absolute consequences of every expression. I mean by this that angry people tend to surround themselves with other angry people. People who lie will be lied to. Fearful people will experience excessive danger or at least the potential for danger wherever they go. People who find fault in others will fill their lives with fault at every turn. On the other hand, people who express joy will experience a world filled with joyous people and circumstances. People who express a genuine love for life will find more and more about which to celebrate. Everyone experiences the reflections of their expressions. We employ in every moment of our lives this perfect balance of the creative process.

As we become more aware of the presence of Spirit in and as everything around us, the judgments that have so many times before swelled up inside will begin transforming into a new sense of peace, tolerance and understanding. As we realize that everyone is Spirit expressing into life and then experiencing the result, any desire to criticize or see others as less than whole will lose its allure.

When other's actions burden us, the burden is what we choose to experience. Seeing everything and everyone as Spirit allows us to release any sense that life can threaten or burden us. Knowing life as the presence of Spirit can actually make it easier because we will no longer need to see the actions of others as being directed at us personally.

Whenever we do not sense this freedom from judgment, we need only remind ourselves that the specific person or circumstance before us is Spirit incarnate. To whatever degree we can embrace this idea, our perceptions will shift, and we will be able to move into a more peaceful or even joyful state of awareness.

Everything around us perfectly reveals the Divine, which to me means that we live in paradise as soon as we choose to make it so. This is a wonderful and extraordinarily powerful way to relate to the fullness and richness of life.

Embracing the Truth

Embracing these principles entails a process of knowing Spirit in a very different way. When we do this, our lives are certain to change. How we experience family and friends, how we relate to our work and even how we see a sunset or hear a bird sing will forever be more meaningful and valuable. Recognizing that nothing is separate from anything else brings us into an ever deepening awareness of the infinite nature and presence of Spirit. Our experience of life becomes our experience of Spirit within and all around us. This knowing invites our hearts and minds to open to the fullness and richness of life as never before, as we are welcomed into this new way of living.

Step One — Recognition

Now, with this foundational understanding of how one can recognize the Oneness of Spirit, you are ready to formulate Step One statements for your Spiritual Mind Treatment.

Your Spiritual Mind Treatments could begin with the phrase "I know." This brings a sense of power and certainty to your opening statement, as opposed to phrases like "I think," "I hope," "I wish," or "I want." When we say, "I know," we demonstrate confidence and conviction in the statement that follows. If you don't begin you first step with "I know," make sure whatever words you use evoke a sense of certainty that what you say is very real for you.

The first step of Spiritual Mind Treatment may be framed as if it was in answer to questions such as these: What do I know about Spirit? Is Spirit truly all there is? Can you see Spirit in all things? Does the entire universe dwell within the Oneness of Spirit? The stronger your statement of recognition, the more powerful the result will be; the more ambiguous the statement, the less effective your Treatment will be.

This chapter ends with a space where you can begin to practice articulating your own personal recognition statement. I invite you to begin this process by taking a moment to clear your mind with a few deep breaths. Then open yourself to the expansiveness of the universe by again asking yourself the question, "What do I know about Spirit?"

Creating Recognition Statements

On the following page, there are five spaces for you to begin developing phrases of recognition. They are intentionally different lengths, each progressively longer. If you need more space, do not hesitate to use paper outside this book. In fact, I invite you to take paper and pen and write dozens or even hundreds of statements that recognize the power and presence of Spirit.

Be bold in your statements. Capture as much of Spirit as you can. Be excited and impressed by this awesome knowingness. Open your heart and your mind as widely as you can. This is your chance to make Spirit bigger than you ever have before. Go for it!

My Recognition Statements

1. _____

2. _____
_____

3. _____
_____
_____

4. _____
_____
_____
_____

5. _____
_____
_____
_____
_____

Ernest Holmes on God / Spirit...

First, I believe that God is Universal Spirit, and by Spirit I mean the Life Essence of all that is – that subtle and intelligent Power which permeates all things and which, in each individual, is conscious mind. I believe that God is Universal Spirit, present in every place, conscious in every part, the Intelligence and mind of all that is.

Can We Talk to God (1934), p. 75.2

God is Life; not some life but all Life. God is Action; not some action but all Action. God is Power; not some power but all Power. God is Presence; not some presence but all Presence. God is pure Spirit, filling all space.

This Thing Called Life (1943), p. 5.5

We believe in God, the Living Spirit Almighty; one, indestructible, absolute and self-existent Cause. This One manifests itself in and through all creation but is not absorbed by its creation. The manifest universe is the body of God; it is the logical and necessary outcome of the infinite self-knowingness of God.

"What We Believe" *Science of Mind* Magazine, (Oct. 1927)

STEP TWO

Identification, Unification

Knowing Ourselves As Spirit

All are but parts of one stupendous whole,
whose body Nature is, and God the Soul.
—ALEXANDER POPE

Who are you? This question forms the foundation for the
second step of Spiritual Mind Treatment. This simple and direct
question is neither about identifying your name or your profes-
sion, nor is it about the attributes you present to the world. It
doesn't concern where you were born or where you live, nor does
it have anything to do with what you have, what you want or
where you are going. This question goes much deeper by asking
you to identify the very essence of your existence.

As compelling a question as this may seem, and though it may
invite you to delve into the inner workings of your mind in
search of a deeply mystical revelation of your true essence, I
suggest the answer is much closer. It has already been provided
in the first chapter of this book. If you embrace the concept that
Spirit is all there is as presented in Step One of Spiritual Mind
Treatment, then the only possible response to the question,
"Who are you?" is that you *must be Spirit.*

Wow, that's a big statement! *You are Spirit.* It's such a big
statement that you shouldn't be surprised if you hear a voice in

25

your head shouting, "No way, I'm not Spirit! I didn't create the Universe." If so, I encourage you to set that argument aside for now and allow yourself an open-minded reading of the next few pages and give these ideas a context in which to reveal their true potential.

Because the idea of knowing yourself as Spirit may be a new concept for you, I invite you to try it on like a brand new, very expensive suit of clothing. Just see how it feels. Perhaps there is something about being Spirit that appeals to you. See if there isn't something about knowing yourself as Spirit that beckons you like an ancient voice calling from a far away place. However you do it, just give these ideas a chance to open you up to an extraordinary new and delightful awareness.

Not much in our outer world supports the outrageous claim that we are all expressing as Spirit in everything we think, say and do. It is much easier to simply accept that we are all separate and individual people, and that each one of us acts independently of everyone or everything else. This "illusion of separateness" seems necessary for us to function in a three-dimensional universe, but at the same time conceals from us the true essence of who we are.

Consider the possibility that before you were born you knew yourself only as Spirit in that you had no sense of being separate from anything. Then at birth, you were suddenly faced with an endless stream of different physical experiences. Feelings of discomfort, hunger, and cold were new and strange sensations for you. Still, for the first few months of your human experience, you continued to make no distinction between yourself and your mother. Then as time passed, you came to accept this new world as the reality of life. Everything, including yourself, appeared to be separate from everything else. With no other known options available, you embraced the idea that you were separate, independent, and only a small insignificant part of the grand scheme of life.

This illusion of separateness continued to become even more pervasive in your thinking. When presented with the idea of a creator of the universe, you could only presume that this creator had created everything as separate, including you. And in the way so many imagine Spirit, you came to believe that this God must spend a great deal of time somewhere else dealing with important matters to which you were not a part. With an entire universe to manage, you could easily have presumed that the Creator could only be available or interested in the most important matters of your life.

From this simplistic scenario, we can understand how easily anyone can come to the seemingly reasonable conclusion that we are completely separate from one another. We can also understand how many hold onto such thinking for an entire lifetime. There is, however, a most amazingly different way of experiencing yourself in relation to Spirit. Let's explore some of these possibilities.

Spirit Expressing and Experiencing As Us

Everything that Spirit does actualizes in only one of two ways: Spirit expresses and Spirit experiences. That's it! And that is all we can do, too. Everything about our lives fits into one of these two actions. When we think, say, or do anything or take any form of outward action, we are expressing into life. When we see, hear, taste, touch, smell, feel, receive or understand anything, or take any form of inward action, we are experiencing life. Through these actions, we are in constant relationship with our environment. And through these actions, Spirit is in constant relationship with Spirit.

Everything comes from Spirit in the form of creative expression, moves through Spirit as Subjective Mind (or Law), and is received by Spirit as the experience of that which is created. This is the cycle of creation, which happens constantly throughout our entire universe. This concept will be further developed in the next chapter. For now, what is important to know is that everything we are exists within the Oneness of Spirit.

Separation and Judgment Working Together

Consider the idea that the One, expressing through you and as you, is indeed the Creator of all life. Consider additionally the idea that what distinguishes you from the next person expressing as Spirit is your outward appearance (physical form) and your personality (mental form). These are the masks we wear to maintain our illusion of separateness.

"But, why would Spirit do so many of the things I have done in my life?" you might ask.

Why not? Whether or not we are happy with the conditions of our lives is no indication of the presence or absence of Spirit.

When we judge our actions by labeling some as "good" (things of which we think God would approve) and some as "bad" (things of which we think God would not approve), then life becomes a complicated matrix of judgments that make living increasingly more difficult, challenging and confusing. We have created, or more likely been given, a limiting self-image that includes ideas of failure and inadequacy, none of which serve us.

However, if these principles which suggest, "Spirit is all that there is" are true, then everything that exists must be an expression of Spirit. Likewise, if Spirit is all that there is, then Spirit is the only presence available to experience those expressions. We as human beings are fully engaged within the divine flow of consciousness. As Spirit expresses through and as you and me, we take what we are experiencing and judge it and assign it to categories of good or bad, right or wrong. We do this to separate and organize our experiences so that we can have a sense of order and safety in our lives. We do this as a culture by making agreements about what is appropriate or acceptable to say or do. We then agree to use these judgment labels collectively to create an even greater sense of order and safety. Ultimately there is nothing absolute about any of our judgments because our perceptions change from circumstance to circumstance. And, our sense of order and safety is nothing more than an illusion that helps us function in a world that plays well to our physical senses.

Even the most intense human expressions cannot be divided into absolute values. For example: Is killing someone a bad or wrong thing to do? The standard of our culture could be summed up as follows: People who kill other human beings for reasons other than self-defense are likely to be punished by incarceration and may even be executed if their state imposes the death penalty on convicted murders. Our culture also says it's acceptable to kill an enemy when defending our country, or our country's interests. So is it right to kill, is it wrong, bad, or good? Even something as important as the taking of human life has moral boundaries that are based on circumstances. Such a lack of absolute values may cause our rules of appropriate moral behavior to seem confusing.

On the other hand, is something as simple as giving someone a box of chocolates a good thing? Well of course it is, unless the recipient is allergic to chocolate, diabetic, struggling with weight control, or generally dislikes such things. Under those conditions it's a bad thing, right? Well except when you consider that it is offered as a sincere gift with the pure intention of expressing love or appreciation. There are so many twists and turns involved in judging what is good and what is bad that there can be no clear black and white determinations. By judging any circumstance or individual, we are attempting to separate that which is being judged from Spirit and ultimately diminishing our awareness of Divine Presence.

When we relate to life in absolute terms, there are no judgments of right or wrong, good or bad. In absolute terms, there is no separation between who you are and what Spirit is.

As human beings we use systems of laws to create balance and appropriateness in our interactions with one another. When someone is determined to have broken a law, misdemeanor or felony, he or she is forced to pay a price either with time, money or possibly even with his or her life. It in no way adds to this process to label anyone good, bad, right or wrong. Prisons are filled with Spirit expressing. Does that mean we like it? Of course not!

One of my closest friends once served time in prison for drug trafficking many years ago. Today he is a shaman who supports people along their spiritual path. You could say he was bad when he was selling drugs and that what he did was wrong, but that would be a limited perception of this man. I prefer to know that he has always been on his path, experiencing exactly what he needed to experience to find his way to the work he is doing today.

There are clearly things that we prefer and seek out, as well as things we avoid and prefer not to have in our lives. However, when we choose not to judge the situations and circumstances of our lives, we are more able to see Spirit in all things. This means that we see Spirit in our difficult times as well as when our experiences are pleasant; we experience Spirit through our pain as well as our pleasure. We recognize the presence of Spirit in our tragedies and failures every bit as much as in our triumphs and successes.

Every part of our lives is filled with the Divine. Can you find Spirit in every aspect of your life? The presence of Spirit is revealed to you as your heart and mind are ready to know this Truth. I claim this for you now!

As a Wave Is To the Ocean

Imagine for a moment a wave as it swells and crashes in the ocean. What is the relationship of that wave to the entire ocean? Actually, they are the same. The wave is an expression of energy within the flow and function of the ocean. The wave is the ocean even though we can see the wave and are unable to see the entire ocean. The ocean and the wave are the same in every way other than size and form. Now, if you consider that the waves represent us, and the ocean represents the wholeness of Spirit, we can see that everything that exists within Spirit exists within you and me. The relationship between the ocean and the wave and between Spirit and you and me is the same. Because we exist within the essence of Spirit, we are able to experience and express life in the same manner, using the same principles of creation with which Spirit experiences and expresses life.

We have within us the innate ability to create our experience in the same way that "all of Spirit" creates the entire universe. The power used to create all of life is the same power we use to create the circumstances of our lives. The ocean expresses as the wave and Spirit expresses as you. It's all the same thing.

Creating On the Inside

The idea that whatever is created by Spirit exists within Spirit, and that there is no outside, may be a different way of experiencing creation. When we create something in physical form, it appears to be separate from us. Experiencing life from a space-time perspective supports the illusion of separateness, albeit a necessary illusion that allows us to function within the physical plane (i.e. having bodies and moving through a linear progression of experiences).

If indeed Spirit is all that there is, then there can be nothing outside of Spirit. There can be only that which is contained within

Spirit. Even in the illusion of separation, everything exists within the Oneness of Spirit.

Other Things to Know About Step Two

Although the second step of a Spiritual Mind Treatment is a vitally important part of the process we are exploring, it does not stand on its own. Inextricably connected to Step One, Step Two has no foundation or substance without it. For this reason, some have found it impossible to fathom the idea of being Spirit. Nonetheless, anyone who resonates with the idea that the Absolute Oneness of Spirit includes everything should be able to begin embracing the Oneness of self and Spirit.

Understanding and living in Oneness is a direction, not a destination. Each day provides an opportunity to delve more deeply into the subtleties of awakening to our true nature. Claiming our Oneness in Spiritual Mind Treatment moves us toward the awareness we seek, carrying us further each day along our path toward enlightenment. This is what we accomplish by evoking Step Two in Spiritual Mind Treatment.

Identification and Unification

It may be helpful to know that different groups use different names for Step Two of Spiritual Mind Treatment. The name we choose to use is not as important as the principle we seek to embody. I use *Identification* because my objective is to identify myself as Spirit. Others use *Unification,* not because they seek to unify with Spirit (we cannot be separate from Spirit), but to unify their awareness of who they are with their awareness of Spirit. Dr. Holmes is said to have used both terms in describing the process of Spiritual Mind Treatment.

What Does It Mean to Know We Are Spirit?

How would your life be different if you knew you were Spirit? How would you begin your day differently? How would you see family members, friends, coworkers and even strangers, knowing that we are all expressing and experiencing as Infinite Spirit? What if whenever you were putting yourself down or questioning your abilities, you were putting down or questioning Spirit? How would you need to change your language and even your thoughts to match your new awareness?

What if you knew whatever you claimed as so, was so? What I mean is that if you had a cold and said out loud believing, "I have vibrant health," then the cold would just cease to exist, and you would have vibrant health. Well, that is exactly the way it works.

This is your true nature. Once the veils of judgment and separation begin lifting, we begin experiencing an intensely joyous connection to all of Life. We can praise and rejoice in all we see, hear, and feel, being aware that everything we know as the truth is already manifest within the Divine essence of Spirit.

Take this sense of potential into the exercises for Step Two. Begin to express the truth within you by clearly knowing that "Spirit and I are One!"

Identification Exercise

To begin, read the statement below. Then close your eyes for a moment and get centered and know that whatever quality you can imagine about Spirit is also a quality that exists within you. Then fill in the blanks until all the statements are complete. Again, be bold and inspired in knowing the truth about you!

Spirit is _____, I am _____.

Spirit is _____, I am _____.

Spirit is _____, I am _____.

Spirit is _____, I am _____.

Spirit is _____, I am _____.

Spirit is _____, I am _____.

Spirit is _____, I am _____.

Spirit is _____, I am _____.

Spirit is _____, I am _____.

Spirit is _____, I am _____.

Spirit is _____, I am _____.

Spirit is _____, I am _____.

Spirit is _____, I am _____.

Spirit is _____, I am _____.

Unification Exercise

Below write three Recognition statements from Step One, either by drawing from your work on page 23, or by coming up with new statements. Then as you write each statement, add a Step Two (Identification/Unification) statement. Make certain that Steps One and Two are in alignment with, and reflective of, one another.

1. _____

2. _____

3. _____

Ernest Holmes on
Identifying/Unifying with Spirit...

We are compelled to think of Spirit either as apart from us or within us. If apart from us, there is no way to find It. If within us, there is no escaping the divine fact.

Living the Science of Mind (1984), p. 12

God is in us. Realizing this indwelling God to be the one and only Life and then sensing our nature as divine is scientific—and it will work wonders.

Questions and Answers on the Science of Mind (1935), p. 96.3

The Spirit is both an over-dwelling and an indwelling Presence. We are immersed in It, and It flows through us as our very life.

Living the Science of Mind (1984), p. 96.7

God is not a person; God is a Presence. That Presence personifies in us as persons. We are personifications of the Infinite on the level of what we call the human being.

10 Ideas That Make a Difference (1966), p. 61.2

STEP THREE

Declaration, Affirmation, Realization
Applying the Truth

Destiny is not a matter of chance, it is a matter of choice:
it is not a thing to be waited for, it is a thing to be achieved.
—WILLIAM JENNINGS BRYANT

Through the process of Spiritual Mind Treatment, we become more aware of our ability to create. We do not need Spiritual Mind Treatment to create because we are already creating all the time. In fact, we live in a constant state of creative expression in which we are continuously manifesting the substance and conditions of our lives. We use Spiritual Mind Treatment to move our creative process out of a subconscious automatic reaction to life and into a conscious and intentional interaction with life.

We begin our exploration of the third step of Spiritual Mind Treatment with a look at the names used to describe it and the meanings behind the names. The first name assigned to the third step is *Declaration*, which Ernest Holmes described as "voicing, in thought, what we desire in some aspect of our lives." By declaring that some condition or outcome exists, we establish it in the Mind of Spirit and allow the creative process to manifest our declaration into physical form.

The second name for the third step is *Affirmation*. The use of this term brings to mind two points. First, when we affirm that

37

some condition or objective already exists, we are asserting a creative influence over its materialization. In other words, if we claim it is so with clarity and conviction, then the universe will support it being so. Second, the root word in Affirmation is "firm," meaning that when we affirm an idea, we are making that idea firm, solid and evident to the physical senses.

The third name for the third step of Spiritual Mind Treatment is *Realization*, which means that we use this step to realize that the Truth of Spirit is greater than the conditions we experience. The idea of Realization involves moving our awareness from the world of physical conditions into the realm of causation. By realizing Truth, we transcend the limitations of physical appearances. When we observe the illusions of illness and poverty, we realize that the natural state of all life is vibrant health and abundance, and we call it forth. By focusing on this Truth, we have the ability to transcend the limitations of physical form and recreate our lives in alignment with the fullness and richness of life.

Regardless of which name you choose, Truth remains constant. Whether you are declaring, affirming or realizing Truth, the outcome we seek already exists in the Mind of Spirit and is available to us according to our beliefs.

The Purpose of Step Three

If you are seeking to resolve a health issue, your Step Three may be to know that excellent vibrant health, the natural state of being for all things, is also your natural state. If you are seeking to heal a relationship, your Step Three may be to know that joy, peace and understanding are the natural states of being in every relationship, including yours. If you are seeking to resolve a financial issue, your Step Three may be to know that you live in an abundant and prosperous world and that having plenty of money to do whatever you desire is the Truth about you. And if you seek to have any particular object or condition in your life, your Step Three could be to know that life always supports you, and your claim for whatever you desire is yours.

How We Create As Spirit

There is a power in the Universe and we use it. We use this power in every moment of every day from our very first breath to our very last. This power is the creative expression of Spirit. In the second chapter of this book, we explored how Spirit is the sum total of all that is and how we dwell within this Oneness. In the third chapter, we learned that we have the ability to create our lives and that we constantly engage in that creative process.

To begin understanding how this creative process occurs, consider the following model offered by Dr. Ernest Holmes in his book, *The Science of Mind* (1926). In this model we find a very simple design that offers some remarkable insights into how we are able to express our lives into physical form.

In using this model, it is important to note that the essence of Spirit cannot be captured in a simple line drawing, and what is offered here is a representative way of depicting the creative process in easily understood terms.

In this model, the circle represents Spirit in the context of Voltaire's words, "God is a Circle . . . whose circumference is nowhere," meaning that nothing can contain Spirit. The circle is used here to represent all of Spirit, that which transcends all space-time and physical form. At the top of this circle is the term Universal Spirit, meaning the creative source, the point of initiation for all energy and physical form. This is the origin of all ideas, notions, revelations and inspirations. It is where all Divine expression originates. It is what causes everything to exist that is, seen and unseen, known and unknown.

In the center of the circle is the area referred to as Universal Subjectivity, which is the medium or means through which all thought moves into a state of material manifestation. Universal Subjectivity or as I like to call it, Universal Law, is the unseen means by which the creative process progresses from an initiating spark into physical form. The term Universal Subjectivity means that the process of manifestation is *subject to* the creative force of Spirit. This Law does not care what is created; it has no agenda, no investment, and no desires. It is always available and responsive to whatever we focus upon.

At the bottom of the Circle, we find the word Manifestation, which represents all things resulting from the creative process. Manifestation is the out-picturing effect of the creative process. This, the body of Spirit, includes all things visible and invisible, all objects, all energy, all motion, all ideas, and every person, place and thing that exists in physical form or otherwise. Here our bodies exist. Here our ideas exist. Here we experience all of life in our multidimensional universe.

Now that I have given you a brief explanation of how Dr. Holmes describes his Metaphysical Chart, I want to offer a simpler version.

At the very moment you have a thought, the creative process has already begun. In the same way a thought is created, the physical world is created. As a thought comes to your mind, you (Spirit) are simultaneously directing the ever-constant, ever-consistent mechanism of subjective mind (Law) into action, bringing into physical form (Body) that which is equivalent to your original thought. This does not mean that if you think about owning a sports car that you will automatically own a sports car. You may also have a thought that you cannot afford to own that kind of car, which counteracts the original idea.

Factors of emotional intensity and degrees of commitment influence the creative process. Still the basic formula of Spirit-Law-Body helps us understand and remember how the process of manifestation works.

Ultimately therefore, whatever we think about is also what is being created.

So what do you think about? As you move through your day, do you think about how beautiful and extraordinary your life is? Do thoughts about the difficulties and frustrations of life control your attention, or do you get excited about the incredible possibilities and opportunities that await you? Do you live in a state of worry or a state of wonder? On what does your mind dwell?

Universal Subjectivity or the Law of Spirit does not care one bit what we direct into existence through our thoughts. Every expression is spiritually valid. The Law's only job is to take the impress of the thoughts we place upon it and bring those thoughts into experiential physical form. Therefore, if we believe people in positions of authority are difficult to deal with, we will find ourselves in difficult situations with people in positions of authority. If we distrust the people around us and worry about being cheated, we will surround ourselves with people who seek to deceive, lie and cheat us. Equally, if we believe that life is precious and everyone we meet is expressing the presence of Spirit, we will again and again experience life according to that belief.

The most powerful idea I believe anyone can take from this model is that nothing is created by anything physical; everything created originates from Spirit in Mind.

In the same way Spirit expresses the cosmos into being, you express your life into being. Your life manifests constantly into physical form and conditions as a result of your thoughts, emotions, and beliefs. As we become more aware of this creative process, we become more responsive to accepting responsibility for the conditions and circumstances of our lives. As a result, we use this responsibility to live more consciously, knowing the world supports us according to our understanding of it.

Truth vs. Fact

When we believe that our present and future are destined to be much the same as what we have experienced in the past, we allow facts to determine the direction of our lives. Go back to the circle for a moment. The lower section of the circle represents the observable universe, where we experience life through our senses. When we experience a condition and accept our experience as truth, we (who are operating from the principles represented in the top section of the circle) create a memory of that condition in Mind.

If the condition is important to us, we assign an emotional link, which intensifies its significance as we store it in our subjective memory. This emotional link may be fear, anger, joy, or any number of other affective states. This results in thinking that the experience represents the truth, and we use this thinking to recreate similar experiences in our lives.

When I was in my twenties, I was racing down a staircase in an office building where I worked. As I pivoted around a landing on the stairs, my right ankle gave way, and I severely injured the ligaments in that ankle to the point that I had to go to a hospital emergency room for x-rays. As a result, I had to walk on crutches for more than a week. For many years after that incident when I would be in a stressful situation, I would manage to twist my ankle on a pebble, or a slippery or uneven floor, or even with no apparent reason and find myself writhing on the ground in pain. What was most bizarre about this situation was that it not only happened to my right ankle, but to my left ankle, as well.

The thoughts I developed around this phenomenon were, "I have weak ankles," and "If there is one stone in a parking lot, I'll walk on it and twist my ankle." And my most profound thought did not even have words. It was simply the memory of feeling my ankle twist and remembering the subsequent pain. Every time this would happen, I could recollect the pain to the point that I would wince as though I was feeling the pain in that moment. All of this perpetuated my condition.

When I began to study metaphysics in my thirties, I devised an affirmation to counteract this condition. My affirmation was simple, "My ankles are strong; my ankles are healthy; my ankles support my weight easily." So any time I had a thought about my ankles twisting or I experienced the memory of that pain, I immediately recited my affirmation. In the last ten years I have twisted my ankle only once. That was on a construction site in the midst of a stressful experience, and I was still able to walk on it within only a couple of minutes of having fallen.

This story illustrates how we create the conditions of our lives through Mind and it is true for every condition. When we experience something and believe "that's just the way life is," we are most likely to create the same experience over and over again. I know a man who over the course of his life had been in three significant relationships and once suggested that his current and former partners must be having clandestine meetings to discuss how to make his life more miserable. It was not a secret conspiracy but rather his own beliefs about himself and his relationships that were creating similar conditions with different partners.

So what are the conditions of your life that keep repeating? Do they have to do with your health, your relationship with money, your employment situation or your intimate relationship or lack of one? Are the facts of your past driving the conditions of your present and influencing the prospects for your future? If you believe in the experiences of your past, you will likely create similar ones in the future.

When we draw our understanding of life from what has happened in the past, we live in the limited reality of facts. However, when we know what is true in the "all of Spirit," we are not limited to creating only that which we have previously experienced. Instead, we are open to creating whatever we can imagine in the unlimited potential of Spirit.

When we use what has happened in our past as our reality, we will likely create the same result as we did in the past. This is an incredibly limited and ineffective way of creating our lives. The truth is that we are in total control of our experience.

Also true is that whatever we experience means whatever we as individuals choose for it to mean. Only you can provide meaning to the events and circumstances of your life. Only I can provide meaning to my life. Everything in your life is actually and ultimately about you. You determine what has value and significance, and you choose what will happen next. The same is true for me. Even so, we face the same question: "What is important to us right now and what do we choose to experience next in our lives?" What we express in thought will determine what we experience in physical form.

Knowing Truth

Spiritual Mind Treatment is about knowing Truth. This is not a relative truth as in your truth or mine. Individual truths are based on facts and only influence our individual realities. The Truth I speak of is unconditional and unchanging. An awareness of Truth requires that you observe the universe in its full and absolute state of existence. When considering "the All of life," we observe that there is a sense of perfect order. The sun comes up every morning; the phases of the moon are always predictable; the seasons change in a consistent fashion; the tides come in and go out on a precise timetable; and the universe always moves in perfect balance.

Nature is constantly demonstrating its abundance. Even after great fires, floods, hurricanes, earthquakes and other such occurrences, plant and animal life always return. We can count the number of seeds in a piece of fruit, but we cannot count the number of potential fruit trees in a single seed. Life's abundance is without limitation. These express the undeniable Truth of life.

When we create from a position of Truth, we create extraordinary and meaningful experiences that expand our consciousness and bless our lives. When we create from a position of fact, we limit ourselves to that which we have already experienced, which is only a small fraction of what life offers.

Understanding Perfection

We live in a culture that teaches us that perfection is highly desirable, and at the same time tells us that it is largely unachievable. The reason is that perfection is defined in our culture as the precise manifestation of all our expectations and desires. For this to be so, for our lives to be perfect, everything would need to appear just as we imagined it would. Anything less and it just isn't perfect. Using this definition of perfection leaves us with nothing ever being good enough, everything always needing to be better. When we connect our expectations to our outcomes, we are always left wanting. What an unfulfilling way to live!

What if, instead of being an elusive desire, perfection was the standard by which all life existed? What if everything was already perfect? Consider for a moment that if Spirit is all there is, and everything exists within the Divine Oneness of Spirit, then everything must already be perfect.

How could this be with all of the pain and suffering in the world? First of all, pain is an inevitable aspect of the human experience. Your body is designed with massive numbers of nerve endings that tell you when you are doing something that damages it. This is a blessing. If we did not have such a system, we would lose our ability to maintain healthy, high-functioning bodies.

Suffering, on the other hand, is not required. We suffer when we fall into the trap of believing that our pain will never end. While pain is a physical experience that has a purpose, suffering is an emotional experience that serves only to intensify itself.

Still, all pain and suffering perfectly express Spirit, as does everything else when we consider that a more accurate understanding of perfection is that Spirit always creates perfectly. And you, expressing as Spirit, can create only perfection. This means that your life is a perfect manifestation of everything you have thought, felt, believed, said and done up to this moment in time. A tree is a perfect manifestation of the potential that existed within the seed from which it came. By using the water, sunlight, air and nutrients that it absorbs, it achieves its full ability to express in physical form. The tree is perfect in the same way that all the conditions and circumstances of our lives are created perfectly out of the seeds of our thoughts.

Traditionally, we learned to use the term "perfect" as a way of acknowledging that all our expectations have been met. "The dinner turned out perfectly; the quarterback threw a perfect pass; what a perfect day." To understand the way we create the conditions of our lives, we use the word perfect in a different way. Perfection is the standard of all creation. This means our expectations have no effect on the perfection of life.

Spirit perfectly expresses as all of creation. When we see that perfection exists all around us, we experience peace with the world. Ours is not to force the world into a submission of perfection, but rather to become evermore aware of the presence of Spirit in everything that we see, hear, taste, smell, feel, and know. Perfection is something of which to become aware, not something to achieve.

Can you see the perfection in your life? Can you see how everything you have ever thought, everything you have said, and everything you have done has created your experience? Some people use the phrase, "You made me do, say, or feel something." This is never true. No one can make us do anything. Likewise, no one can keep us from saying and thinking whatever we choose.

There are circumstances under which our bodies can be controlled. An example would be when US military personnel have been held as prisoners of war. Even in such extreme conditions, what those individuals thought, said, and felt during their captivity was completely their choice. We have always had the right and ability to think, say, and feel whatever we choose, even though at times there may have been unpleasant consequences that resulted. To believe otherwise is limited thinking that results in our reacting to life rather than powerfully and effectively interacting with life.

You are indeed perfect. Everything about your life is perfect. This does not mean that you have to like your life the way it is; however, it does serve you to know that you create your life and that creation is always a work in progress. If you would like to change some "perfect" condition that you no longer desire into another more preferable perfect condition, all you have to do is know that it is so, then act accordingly. This is what Spiritual Mind Treatment is all about.

Never Ask, Always Know

Spiritual Mind Treatment is a form of affirmative prayer, and in no way petitions anyone for anything. If we experience Spirit as all there is, whom would we be asking to provide us with something? Who would be making the decisions as to whether we should or should not receive what we request? The power of Spirit exists equally at every point. There is nothing outside of us that has a greater or lesser presence of Spirit than us. When we accept this understanding, we claim our sacred birthright within the Oneness of Spirit.

Spiritual Mind Treatment is an exercise in knowing who we are. When we know Spirit as All, we cannot help but understand that we exist within this Oneness. When we know the Truth of Spirit, we know the Truth of ourselves.

Asking implies that there is a power separate from us that we must appeal to before we can receive a desired outcome. Knowing implies that the power of Spirit is within and all around us, available for our use right now. When doing Spiritual Mind Treatment, we first know the Truth, then claim it as our own and use it as our guiding force.

The Four Elements of Step Three

To make our Spiritual Mind Treatments most effective, there are four elements to address in Step Three. When we know the Truth of Spirit in the absolute, we realize that the same Truth applies specifically to us in these four ways:

1. PERSONAL: We know that this Truth also applies to our specific lives, so it is Personal.

2. PRESENT: We know that Spirit, as creative cause, operates right here and right now, so we know that the Truth of us happens in the Present, regardless of our ability to see the immediate effect.

3. POSITIVE: We know that Spirit is creative, not destructive, so we realize that Truth is Positive in nature. This means that we focus on what we choose to experience rather than whatever we do not want to experience.

4. PRECISE: We know that life reflects our thoughts back to us specifically according to our beliefs, so we state the Truth of Spirit in Precise terms that apply directly to our lives.

When these four elements are present, our third step of treatment will be clear and powerfully reflected in the Mind of Spirit. Below we will explore these four elements by learning their importance and what makes them work.

Make It Personal

When doing Spiritual Mind Treatment for yourself, it is important that you state your treatment in terms of you. Know the Truth about yourself by focusing on the qualities that you desire to experience rather than what someone else has, does or knows.

If you are treating for a relationship, know the Truth about what you seek to experience in this relationship. Do not treat for another person to relate to you in a certain way. How others relate to you is about them, not about you. Your treatment could be for you to be in a loving, fulfilling, meaningful relationship. I know a man who treated to be in relationship with a certain woman, thinking that she would bring with her all the qualities he desired. The treatment worked, but once the relationship began, he was disappointed because she did not bring to the relationship what he expected.

In your personal treatment, avoid making any reference to anyone doing anything. Instead, know the Truth about yourself. You could say, "I have the perfect new car," rather than, "My employer buys me the perfect new car." If you know you have the perfect new car, you are open to having the car by whatever means the universe reflects it into your life. If in your treatment you state that your employer buys you a car, you severely limit the means by which the car can manifest. You are requiring that the consciousness of your employer be in alignment with yours. This limits your likelihood of manifesting the car. Always treat precisely at the point of you. Your treatment is about how you express yourself and how you experience the world. Make it personal and allow it to happen for you.

Stay in the Present

Some people find this element of Step Three challenging. When we do a Spiritual Mind Treatment, we desire to manifest the Truth in our lives, right? In our culture we tend to speak in terms of the future, but the creative process does not happen in the future. The only time we can initiate any manifestation is in the present. The past is gone and there is absolutely nothing we can do in the future. What we have is right now, and there's nothing more powerful than to be fully present in this now moment.

If our Spiritual Mind Treatments are directed toward something happening in the future, we create a mental barrier between where we are today and where we want to be. We do this every time we say, "I want . . ." or, "I need. . . ." When we want or need something, we create a wanting or a needing rather than a having. By using words like want, need, hope, try, or any other word that implies a distancing between our current condition and that which we desire, we actually add to the illusion of separation.

We can effectively keep our treatments in the present by using the word "now." When we say, "I now have . . ." or " I now know . . ." we locate ourselves in time and space in such a way as to focus on and intensify our creative power. The now moment is the only place where anything happens. Claiming our place in the present moment gives us claim to the creative force of life.

Make It Positive

The idea of making our third step statements positive is not about making them happy or uplifting. Being positive means that we focus on what we desire, not on what we do not desire. Never treat for something to go away or for something to cease to exist.

Remember, we create whatever we focus upon. So when we focus on getting rid of whatever we desire to have out of your lives (i.e., a person, circumstance, or whatever we believe no longer serves us), that focus actually holds our connection to exactly that which we want to have gone.

However, when we focus upon that which we desire to bring into our lives, our focus actually supports the manifestation process. So, give energy to that which you desire, and give no attention at all to anything contrary.

When we speak our third step in positive terms, we've chosen to move forward in our lives. When we move forward, a much greater probability exists that we will arrive somewhere other than where we have been.

State your realization in positive terms.

Make It Precise

Spiritual Mind Treatment is not simply a process for claiming whatever you want. To use treatment effectively, you must have a clear understanding of what changes best serve you and the world around you. Treating for a relationship with a certain person may result in just such a relationship; however, this kind of treatment offers absolutely no indication as to whether or not such a relationship will result in an outcome that is fulfilling for you or the other person. Treating for a relationship that is loving, nurturing, joyous, and fun may result in an even more desirous relationship.

When we are precise about the qualities we desire and believe that we have the right and ability to experience them, and we set no limitations on how the universe reflects these qualities into our lives, we are open to the unlimited possibilities of infinite Spirit. The more clearly we express those qualities in our treatment, the more precisely the universe will respond.

Identifying Your Outcome

It's time to begin practicing the realization of Truth about you. What in life calls to you? Is there some form of healing you desire? Would you like a more meaningful relationship or a stronger connection with your partner? Or, is there something more tangible like a new car or home you are looking for? What part of your life are you ready to change? Only you can know what change in condition is best for you, and this is the time to realize the Truth that applies to its full and complete manifestation.

Remember to use the four elements of realization: Make it Personal (I, me), Present (now), Positive (focus on what you want, not what you don't want), and Precise (focus on the qualities of that one condition). Remember that you are not asking for anything, you are claiming the Truth about yourself. By knowing that the words you say are so, your statement and belief will indeed manifest into physical form. Write your words with certainty and clarity. Then say them out loud with enthusiasm and conviction.

When you know the Truth and speak the Truth about yourself nothing can stop you. Do it now.

Your Statement of Realization

Ernest Holmes on
Declaration/Affirmation/Realization...

Everyone automatically attracts to himself just what he is. He should definitely, daily (using his own name) declare the Truth about himself, realizing that he is reflecting his statements into Consciousness and they will be operated upon by It.

The Science of Mind (1938), p. 295.5

It is only when we live affirmatively that we are happy. It is only when we recognize that the universe is built on affirmations that we can become happy.

A Holmes Reader for All Seasons (1993), p. 62

Thought which is built upon a realization of the Divine Presence has the power to neutralize negative thought, to erase it, just as light has the power to overcome darkness; not by combating darkness, but by being exactly what it is: LIGHT.

The Science of Mind (1938), p. 183.2

Gratitude, Acceptance

Expressing Authentic Gratitude

If the only prayer you ever prayed was "Thank You,"
that would suffice.

—MEISTER ECKHART

Congratulations! If you've completed the readings and exercises to this point, you've accomplished the most challenging aspects of using Spiritual Mind Treatment. If you have come to embrace the ideas that Spirit is all there is, that you exist wholly within the Oneness of Spirit, and that through your thoughts you can create whatever you choose, then you have begun the journey of boundless freedom in which you can fully express and experience the purpose and meaning of your life.

There are two remaining steps we will explore in completing our study of the Spiritual Mind Treatment process. Each brings a significant and powerful element that will supercharge our treatments.

The first three steps of Spiritual Mind Treatment are about how we perceive the world and ourselves. Our *recognition* of Spirit, our *identification* of ourselves as Spirit, and our *declaration, affirmation or realization* of the Truth of Spirit all involve cognitive processes. As we move into Step Four we call upon our emotional body to bring an additional dimension, a heart connection to our treatment. Step Four is about gratitude and acceptance. It is about opening our hearts to the beauty of what we know in Truth and creating a resonance with that beauty.

To understand the value of Step Four, we must first look at how we use gratitude in our lives each day and how that differs from the gratitude we seek to generate in our treatment work.

Pitfalls of a Polite Culture

Just about everyone expresses gratitude. It's the polite thing to do. We say "thank you" to servers in restaurants, to clerks in stores, and to virtually anyone who provides us with anything from material goods to advice or information. Gratitude has become a standard of civility, a normal occurrence of our daily lives. Even though on the surface this may seem to be a wonderful custom, I will offer three reasons why I believe saying "thank you" may have lost some of its intended relevance in our culture.

First, whenever we repeat an action so habitually that the act becomes unconscious and possibly even mundane, its value is severely diminished and may even be eliminated. We are left with polite words that are void of meaning and significance.

Second, when someone expects a response of gratitude and it is not forthcoming, they may have an adverse reaction such as feeling unappreciated or seeing the offender's omission as selfish and uncaring. When anyone expects an expression of gratitude and reacts to not receiving it, he or she may foster an illusion of separation. What results is that we say "thank you" throughout each day, not because we mean it, but because it is expected of us.

And although more subtle, my third and final reason may have the most insidious effect on our well-being. When we say "thank you," we are implying some degree of contentment in the moment and in life generally. And even though we say "thank you" all day long, we may not actually be content with the significant circumstances of our lives. This creates tension. When this is so, the quantity and quality of material possessions does not seem to matter, nor does how intact any family may be, nor how successful a career may be; we may still feel hooked by an inner feeling of discontentment or incompleteness. Saying we are grateful while at the same time having such feelings of discontentment creates a tension that perpetuates and magnifies any sense of dissatisfaction. Ultimately, this tension becomes suffering, and suffering leads to disease and desperation and being far away from the happiness and contentment we all desire.

I am not suggesting that we stop saying "thank you" or any other expression of gratitude. On the contrary, I am offering us all an opportunity to play a higher game. How would our experience of relating to others be different if every time we said "thank you," we consciously and genuinely meant it? When we are automatic and unconscious in our expressions of gratitude, we miss the opportunity of experiencing our Oneness. When we are intentional and authentic in our gratitude, we create constant connections to the world around us.

Choosing Gratitude Over Expectations

Think for a moment about how you have at one time or another made a problem bigger than it needed to be. We have all taken an event and used it to throw a cloud of discontent over everything important to us. Whenever expectations do not match experiences, we too often send our lives into a tailspin of upset, resentment or depression. It is as though life is only worth living so long as nothing goes wrong.

A state of discontent has never fostered anything except greater degrees of discontent. We constantly create whatever it is we are focusing on. No matter how much money or creature comforts we may have, our sense of being content comes from how we perceive ourselves and how we relate to the world around us.

When used consciously, expectations can be a useful tool for visioning our lives into fullness. What is important to understand is that when something other than our precise expectation occurs, the value of whatever we experience will always contain within it a revelation of Truth about who we are in Spirit. We hide from the Truth when we move into a state of discontentment. We embrace the Truth when we are aware that the perfection of Spirit dwells in every circumstance and condition of our lives.

The simplest and most effective way I have found to identify the Truth in challenging circumstances is to express authentic gratitude. When I open my heart widely and trust that my life is a perfect expression of Spirit, I cannot help but see myself and the purpose and meaning of my life more clearly. I always expect my life to unfold according to my dreams and desires; yet I do not hold those expectations as the final authority of the perfection of Spirit. Every circumstance and condition I experience fits perfectly into the tapestry of my life. How this is so is revealed to me through my gratitude.

The Power of Gratitude

Our gratitude, in a powerful way, allows us to see the value in any situation, no matter how difficult or troubling it may seem. When we experience a catastrophic circumstance in our lives, our immediate reaction will be to want the problem to go away. Yet, within these circumstances the deepest meanings and most profound understandings of life always reveal themselves.

Having known several parents who have lost young children, I have observed a disparity of response. Some find their way to a place of deep inner peace, where in reflection they can say that losing their child was the most important and meaningful experience of their lives. While others have chosen to continue experiencing the suffering of their loss for many years, perhaps even the rest of their lives. The distinction between the two groups is that the parents who are at peace have chosen to focus on how losing their beloved child calls them to live their lives as fully as possible, while those who are suffering have chosen to focus only on what they have lost.

I know people who have had cancer and relate to it as the most profound and meaningful experience of their lives, and I have met people who have chosen to fear the cancer in their bodies and become victims to it. From these observances, I have come to understand that those who bless their experience of cancer and watch intensely for the value it brings to their lives often gain extraordinary insights and a fresh and abiding appreciation for life.

We choose where we go in life. We can choose to travel a road of significance and use the gift of gratitude in an authentic way to deepen and broaden our experience of life as a meaningful and purposeful journey.

Directing Our Gratitude

Perhaps the most powerful emotional tool we have is authentic gratitude. To move into a state of authentic gratitude, we claim and embrace the presence of Spirit, no matter how the circumstances of our lives may appear. We often use words to express gratitude, but authentic gratitude may transcend language. It can be a knowingness that brings with it a sense of peace and contentment, which permeates the very being of everyone who uses its great power.

When we express authentic gratitude for the conditions, circumstances and relations of our lives, we open ourselves to more fully seeing the gifts of Spirit that surround and permeate our every moment.

FIRST, GIVE THANKS FOR THAT WHICH YOU AFFIRM

When we practice Spiritual Mind Treatment, we recognize the presence of Spirit, we identify ourselves within the Oneness of Spirit, and we realize the Truth of the circumstances of our lives. We realize this Truth, even before we experience the physical manifestation of that which we desire. And although we have done this powerful mental work, it might not take much for us to slip into a state of fearing that what we have proclaimed may not ever materialize. To avoid sabotaging our treatment in this way, we must maintain the energy of our realization by knowing without hesitation that *it already exists*. The most effective way of doing this is to give thanks for it.

We only give thanks for what we already have. Have you ever given thanks for something you didn't have? Probably not. It's not natural. You may thank someone for promising to do something that they have not yet done, but it is the promise for which gratitude is given, not the act yet to come. Realizing one's vibrant health with perfect circulation and easy movement in Step Three of a treatment is significantly enhanced and magnified by a fourth step that gives thanks for a body that is strong, balanced, and healthy in every way.

Stating your gratitude in a Spiritual Mind Treatment seals your realization. It's the icing on the cake. What you have declared to be so is so because you have received it and given thanks for it. Your claim on that which you affirm is solid and unquestioned because you have wrapped it in a blanket of authentic gratitude.

NEXT, GIVE THANKS FOR THAT WHICH YOU NOW HAVE

Being grateful for what we are declaring in Truth demonstrates great power. Still, we can expand on our gratitude to make our Spiritual Mind Treatment even more powerful and effective.

When we focus on manifesting something new in our lives, we tend to deprecate the object or circumstance we want to replace. Doing this actually gets in the way of our having what we desire. If we desire a more reliable or attractive vehicle, we may be looking with great dissatisfaction upon our current means of transportation. When we do this, we are likely giving more energy and attention to not liking that old car than we are to having a new one.

When we can genuinely be grateful for our current situation, we free ourselves to focus all our creative energy on that which we desire. Holding on to a state of discontentment creates a resistance to receiving something greater. Being at peace with where we are and with what we have creates an environment that easily allows us to simply have more.

You've heard the phrase, "To borrow money, you need to have money." From a metaphysical perspective, this is because if you have money, you are already comfortable with having it; so having more is easily accomplished. The same perspective applies in your treatment work. If you are okay with where you are, you can easily manifest something even greater.

I encourage you to include in your treatment a brief statement of authentic gratitude for the blessings that exist in your life right now. By doing this you will be clearing the way for receiving your new manifestation.

FINALLY, GIVE THANKS FOR THAT WHICH BROUGHT YOU HERE

When we recognize Spirit and know that our lives are a Divine expression of this One Spirit, we must also recognize that all of life has always been a Divine journey. Spirit did not just show up one day. Everything we have thought, said and done throughout our lives is an expression of Spirit. So, by acknowledging in gratitude the journey that has brought us to here, we are "knowing" the absolute presence of Spirit in all that we are and in all that we have experienced. Our gratitude is now complete.

Immersing Ourselves In Gratitude

Expressing gratitude is not only powerful; it can also be fun. Take some time here to think about your life. For what are you truly grateful? What are you creating right now in your life for which you are sincerely and authentically thankful? What is it about your life right now that calls for you to say, "Thank You"? Can you look back upon the course of your life and see the value and meaning in where you have been and in what you have done? Can you see how where you are right now is the perfect demonstration of your journey to this point?

Take some time now to reflect on these questions and write down your thoughts. From this you will learn that when you are in touch with the extraordinary journey that is your life and when you can express authentic gratitude for this life, you will more deeply sense the power you wield. By using gratitude as a spiritual tool, you will learn how to propel your life into new and wondrous directions.

I wish you an exciting and extraordinary journey.

Authentic Gratitude Exercise

As you do your exercise, remember that the most important part of this work is what is happening inside you. As you write, be aware of what is happening to you physically and emotionally. Feel yourself lightening and expanding as you move through this exercise.

Write down at least 24 different things that you are grateful for in your life today:

1. _____	13. _____
2. _____	14. _____
3. _____	15. _____
4. _____	16. _____
5. _____	17. _____
6. _____	18. _____
7. _____	19. _____
8. _____	20. _____
9. _____	21. _____
10. _____	22. _____
11. _____	23. _____
12. _____	24. _____

Now go back to the previous chapter and review your Step Three Statements. Then write statements of authentic gratitude from each of these perspectives:

1. How are you grateful for that which you have declared, affirmed, and realized?
2. How are you grateful for the conditions of your life right now?
3. How are you grateful for the presence of Spirit in your life?

Ernest Holmes on Gratitude...

The reason we can make our requests known with thanksgiving is because we know from the beginning that we are to receive and therefore we cannot help being thankful. This grateful attitude to the Spirit puts us in very close touch with power and adds much to the reality of the thing that we are dealing with.

Creative Mind and Success (1919), p. 24.2

Gratitude is one of the chief graces of human existence and is crowned in heaven with a consciousness of unity.

The Science of Mind (1938), p. 497.2

Praise and thanksgiving are affirmations of the Divine Presence, the Divine abundance and the Divine givingness.

A Holmes Reader for All Seasons (1993), p. 62

STEP FIVE

Release

Releasing is Receiving

Let go and let God.

—A.A. SLOGAN

"The only way it's ever going to get done is if I do it myself."
Have you ever said these words? More importantly, have you
ever felt this way? It's easy to think this way when you have
strong expectations about how things should happen. The
problem with doing everything yourself is that the only things
that will ever get done are the things that you have time and
energy to do. Even with the greatest of intentions, doing everything ourselves as individual human beings can often seem ineffective and difficult.

If you're reading this book, chances are strong that you want
your life to work. Doesn't everybody? Well no, there are many
people who have given up on life; they see themselves as failures
and hold no hope for achieving anything of substance or
meaning in this lifetime. This is not true for you. No doubt, there
are some parts of your life that really work, and there is a good
chance that these are the parts you believe are within the realm
of your control.

Yet, the parts of our lives that we can effectively oversee and
manage are only a small portion of our whole experience of

being human. This is true even on the physical plane. For example, when we go to the grocery store, we buy products from all over the world. Produce comes from fruit orchards and vegetable farms, dairy products from dairy farms, fish from fishermen and so on. How many of those products would we eat if we had to grow or catch them ourselves? Not many.

Our use of Subjective Mind works much the same way. When we limit the potential for our treatment based on what we know and can do ourselves, we end up with few options. This would be like trying to grow all the food we were going to eat in our backyards. But when we avail ourselves of all the possibilities; that would be like walking into the grandest most magnificent supermarket in the world. The possibilities are limitless.

To have all these possibilities available to us, we must let go of any predetermined ideas about how our manifestation will occur. We do this by applying the fifth step of Spiritual Mind Treatment, which is the fine art of release.

Releasing your treatment is not about turning the outcomes of your life over to just anyone. The Fifth Step is about getting out of the way and allowing the "all of Spirit" to reflect the Truth back to us, unencumbered by our limited thoughts and beliefs.

"How" is None of Your Business

When we limit the way life works to only what we can do ourselves, we limit our awareness of Spirit. When we believe that things can only happen a certain way, we are saying that the only resources available to us in life are the ones we know about and know how to use. There is so much more to life than any one person can know.

No matter how much we learn in life, we can never know all the means and methods by which Spirit manifests. When we realize the Truth about any condition or circumstance, the greatest power we have is in knowing that our realization is true. If however, within our treatments we include some plan for how our manifestation should occur or from what source it should materialize, we are simply getting in the way and limiting the full power and potential of Universal Law.

This does not mean that when we do treatment work, we should just sit back waiting for something to materialize before us. On the contrary, we take whatever action is appropriate to bring our treatment into physical form and at the same time know that whatever needs to happen for Truth to be revealed has already occurred. We participate in the creative process without limiting the process to our own actions.

Divine Presence exists inherently within us, which means that we always know what to do. We have an innate wisdom within us that guides us through life. Sure, we have all made choices that result in painful or confusing outcomes. Those are the choices that call us to awaken to our inner power and potential. Those are the choices that prepare us for the easier, more rewarding choices we will make now and in the future. All our choices guide us to a place where we are able to more fully understand our world and ourselves.

Spiritual Mind Treatment contains within it an element of choice. When we treat, we recognize the presence of Spirit, and we choose to live our lives in that state of conscious awareness. We choose to be true to our divine nature, we choose clarity of action, and we choose to be open to all the possibilities of Spirit.

Beyond the limitations of our physical being, how Spirit works is none of our business. Neither you nor me nor anyone else can fully understand the mechanics of Divine Mind. And it really doesn't matter how Spirit works anyway. It is not important nor is it necessary for anyone to know all the details of how anything comes into being. What is important is to recognize that you not only have the ability to direct the experiences of your life, but that you have always had this ability and have always used it. This is true whether or not you can understand or explain how it works.

Consider Your Use of "Why?"

One of the ways we attempt to control our lives is by asking "Why?" "Why does this always happen to me?" "Why did he or she do that to me?" "Why can't I get what I want?" These may seem like reasonable questions on the surface, however by asking them, they actually anchor you to that which you claim you do not want. Whatever it is that you are focusing upon is precisely what you are giving energy to and creating in your life. Whatever your attention is focused upon, regardless of whether you are in favor of or opposed to it, what you are doing is supporting its existence in consciousness and perpetuating its existence and expansion.

No answer to any "Why?" question is ever complete. Answers to "Why?" are always conditional and static. When I hear someone ask "Why?" I often think to myself and sometimes even say outloud, "Every answer to 'Why?' is a lie." This is because every answer to "Why?" represents a limited perspective and is never the whole picture.

Children ask "Why?" questions all the time because they are seeking to understand their physical universe. But as adults seeking spiritual understanding, "Why?" provides no real answers; it only holds us to the focus point of the question.

So, I invite you to change your thinking around the words how and why. Neither can offer the power of your trust in Spirit. Instead, recognize that Spirit is all there is, see yourself within the Oneness, affirm the Truth clearly, give thanks, and let it go. When you do this with clarity and focus, the results will amaze you.

The Natural Act of Letting Go

In some ways, letting go comes to us easily and naturally; we do it all the time. Before we take a breath, we always have to release the breath we took before. We don't think about it, we just breathe out and release the air in our lungs. In much the same way, we also constantly release our thoughts. All day long thoughts come to us and we let them go. These are not often original or profound ideas, just passing thoughts about what is important to us, like the things we think need to get done today. We see these passing thoughts as insignificant, but they are not. We build our lives out of them, forming and organizing our reality as we go.

Through our ability to let go, we have immense power to create our reality. We organize our lives with the little thoughts that we think and release all day long. When those little thoughts are about how we cannot be, do or have something, we are building walls of separation between our desired outcomes and ourselves. It does not matter how much we want something. If we believe and release the little thoughts that say we can't be, do or have something, then we can't.

In the same way, when we declare the Truth, believing it is so, then release it just as we would any other thought, we engage Universal Law, which reflects that Truth back to us. Life works the same way regardless of whether we believe we can or cannot be, do, or have anything. It is completely up to each of us to choose for ourselves what life will reflect back to us. We do this by releasing our thoughts, believing in them, and letting them be so.

Making Peace With Current Conditions

We are such powerful beings. We influence the world with every thought and emotion we express. Yet so much of what we create, we claim not to want. We are like creation machines set on *high*. One way we do this is by lamenting the conditions of our lives and at the same time focusing on and reinforcing exactly what we don't want. It is fully within our power to stop this cycle of discontent. We can do this by making peace with the existing conditions of our lives.

The conditions of our lives are the conditions of our lives.

That simply is what's going on. This is not about denying the realities of life; it is about not having any emotional attachment to the conditions we do not want. When we are detached from what we don't want, we are free to live our lives as though the conditions we desire are already present.

For example, if you injure your arm and it is painful for you to move it, you can do a treatment to know you are in excellent health and that your arm functions perfectly and moves easily. Once you have realized the Truth, you can let go of the pain, meaning that you stop focusing on it. Instead, focus on how well your arm moves and how quickly you're healing. This will facilitate a quick and easy healing process. I'm not suggesting you should ignore or deny the pain. Just don't make it the center of your focus. When you focus on the pain, the pain persists. When you focus on the healing, the healing manifests. Let go of the problem and focus on the solution.

In exactly the same way, if you are realizing the Truth about having a new car, focus on how easily you get to wherever you are going in your current transportation. Don't spend any time being frustrated and dissatisfied with your old car. That will only keep the experience of your old car in your way. See yourself in that new car, let go of all emotional attachment to your old car, and the means for you to acquire your new car will reveal itself to you with ease and clarity.

The Power of Letting Go

The Truth is that we are One with all of Spirit, and thus hold within ourselves the full potential of the Divine Infinite. Yet at a conscious level, we have a limited perception of the workings of the Universe. We know some things, but there is so much more that we do not know. Our ability to create is unquestioned, but to be fully empowered in our creative process, we must engage the "All of Spirit" by letting go. The way we do this is by knowing that Spirit is all there is, seeing ourselves within that "allness," affirming the Truth before us, accepting that Truth in gratitude, and releasing it without reservation.

The process of release accomplishes two distinct outcomes. First, by releasing your Spiritual Mind Treatment, you are getting out of the way and allowing the full potential of your realization to manifest into being. Your release frees your demonstration to manifest by any and all methods or means, even those of which you could not possibly be consciously aware.

When you release your treatment, you are releasing the creative process into full expression. All of Spirit is now available to provide unlimited combinations of events, participants, circumstances, and possibilities that will work in Divine order to manifest whatever you have claimed in Truth. Most of this potential exists beyond our ability to imagine. It occurs in precise balance and timing to provide the perfect out-picturing of your demonstration. By releasing, you are opening up and allowing all the power and potential of Divine Spirit to support you and to express your desires into physical form.

Second, when you let go of your realization, you are creating a space in which your manifestation can and will fully materialize. The Universe will not tolerate any void or vacuum. Your letting go actually creates a tension between your realization and that which can be confirmed by the senses in time and space. Letting go works like a magnet to bring into being that which you claim in Truth.

If you believe that what you say is so, then let it go. The result will be the full manifestation of your desires.

Exercising Our Ability To Let Go

Do not underestimate the importance of this step in you Spiritual Mind Treatment work. As you finish your treatment, your mind may well want to return to the "problem." For your treatment to be effective, your release statement must be more powerful and convincing than your desire to worry or any urge you may have to focus on the existing condition. Use your release statements as a way of turning your desire over to the all of Spirit and be vigilant in letting go of any attachment to the result you desire.

Release Exercise

It is time to begin putting words to the idea of letting go. Below I have given you one release statement as an example. This statement is followed by spaces for you to write three additional statements of release. Make each statement strong and clear, and as you write each one, feel the sense of freedom that letting go brings to your treatment. Also, you may want to end each statement with the phrase, "And so it is." In Spiritual Mind Treatment work, these words are comparable to saying "Amen." It is a way of acknowledging to yourself that your treatment is complete.

Example:

"I now release my treatment into the all of Spirit with absolute certainty knowing that these words I say are Truth, and so it is!"

1. _____

2. _____

3. _____

Ernest Holmes on Releasing...

What we outwardly are, and what we are to become, depends upon what we are thinking, for this is the way we are using Creative Power. The sooner we release our minds from the thought that we have to create, the sooner we shall be able to work in line with Spirit.

The Science of Mind (1946), p. 140.4

I let the Spirit take care of the Universe and my affairs, while I release all responsibility... and I am at peace.

The Science of Mind (1946), p. 256.5

I have no responsibility except to create the right kind of a mental receptivity. That is the truth. Thus we, who are seeking to demonstrate, we know that all we have got to do is to realize the truth, that is, use the mind in a positive formative way and the Mind, or the power which creates everything and projects it, will do the rest for us. Until we come to the point where we see that this is all we have to do, it is all thought; no matter how hard we struggle; we could not do anything else.

Love and Law (2001; teachings 1918-1920), p. 46.1

Bringing it All Together

*Whoever should say to this mountain, Be moved
and fall into the sea, and does not doubt in his heart,
but believes that what he says will be done,
it will be done to him.*

—JESUS OF NAZARETH

Spiritual Mind Treatment is a magnificently powerful and effective tool. With the use of these five steps, we can direct our creative energies into any situation that may arise. If you choose to use Spiritual Mind Treatment as a spiritual discipline, it is important for you to understand the methods by which it can be most useful. Each step offers an essential ingredient in the formulation of your treatment. Each step is a piece of a grand design that creates wholeness through spiritual action, the results of which allow us to resolve any conflict, heal any wound, achieve any outcome, or fill any void in our lives.

Experience shows that if we leave out any one of these steps, the effectiveness of our treatments diminishes. A synergistic and progressive order pertains to the five steps of treatment, each one building on the one before and preparing for the one to follow, right through to your closing words, "And, so it is!"

Now that we have explored the fundamental use of each of the five steps, we can also connect the steps in ways that will create a flow of consciousness that transforms them into a complete and seamless treatment. We will achieve in this chapter the ability to express our treatments as a unified whole rather than as a series of parts. By mastering this aspect of our treatments, we achieve greater continuity between the intention and the outcome from our prayers.

Some who do treatment work develop patterned phrases for steps one and two which they memorize and use to begin every treatment. There is nothing wrong with this approach, however, I find it essential in my treatment work to be consciously present in the moment, to remember my Oneness of Spirit, and then to bring this awareness as completely as possible into my thoughts and words. I seldom begin a treatment with the same phrase. This keeps me from falling into a routine and keeps my treatments fresh and focused.

As you begin your treatment, you will have predetermined the Truth to be proclaimed in the third step. That's why you're doing the treatment. To prepare for the full expression of that affirmation/realization, begin addressing it at the very beginning of your treatment.

If you are treating for physical healing, begin your first step by knowing that everything is healed and healthy within the Oneness of Spirit. Know that vibrant health is the natural state of all life. Then moving into step two, know that the healing energy of Spirit exists wholly within you right now because all of Spirit is present in you, as you right now!

If you are treating for understanding, begin by recognizing the omniscience, all knowingness of Spirit. Then, identify yourself with the unity of Divine Mind, knowing that you have absolute access to whatever you seek to understand.

Once you've stated your first three steps, move into expressing your gratitude by continuing the same consistent theme. Give thanks for that which you have affirmed, keeping your treatment focused and on purpose. You may choose to include a brief statement of gratitude for all the blessings of your life, but you will still want your words of thanksgiving to reflect largely upon the intention of your treatment.

Keeping the final step of your treatment in alignment and on purpose with the preceding steps is also important. As you acknowledge the truth of your words and as you release them, stay connected with the power of your words and actions in the treatment.

When our treatments have a constant theme running through each step, we create a powerful and expanding flow of consciousness that builds throughout the process. Everything in our treatments connects and focuses like a laser beam on the manifestation of that Truth we seek to experience. When we use the five steps as a unified force, the creative power of Divine Mind brings that which we focus upon into physical form.

If you use these steps and believe with all your heart and know with your entire mind that the words you say are so, then whatever you desire *must* appear in your life. This is the absolute Law of Attraction. This is how you can use Spiritual Mind Treatment to bring everything about your life into conscious alignment with Truth. There is nothing magical about this process; you have always been creating the experiences of your life. The difference now is that you will do it consciously.

See your treatment as a single expression of Spiritual Truth where five steps become one seamless flow of conscious knowing. Allow treatment to become your tool for guiding your conscious mind into a state of remembering that which you have always known: Spirit is the source of all creation, existing right here, right now in you, as you and through you, and Truth realized is Truth manifest, sealed with gratitude and released into full expression. What a glorious way to move through life. The gift of Spiritual Mind Treatment is your guide to a life ever joyously expanding toward the fullest expression of Spirit. Use it as much and as often as you can. Your life will be richer for it.

It's now time to write a whole treatment for yourself. If this causes you to feel some tension in your body, good! That means you are really going to do this. So, just relax, take a few deep breaths, and know that this is a way of giving yourself a gift. You cannot make a mistake here. There is a prayer in you that wants to reveal itself, and what you are about to do is find it and give it life in the world of ideas that form your life.

Wherever you are, all you need is a pen or pencil. If you prefer not writing in the book (although what a great place to pen your very first written treatment), just find some paper. Any paper will do.

Now as you finish this paragraph, prepare to close your eyes and allow yourself to know what it is that calls you to treatment. Begin by knowing that the condition or circumstance you seek is the Truth about Spirit. Know that if it is so for Spirit, it is also so for you. Clearly state what you know to be the Truth about the condition or circumstance you hold in mind. Give thanks for this knowing and let it go.

Do it now.

My First Spiritual Mind Treatment

Congratulations, you've done it! You're on your way to achieving a richness of experience that has been waiting for you. You are now taking the helm as conscious director of your life. As you continue to expand your ability to consciously create the life you will become and less willing to live your life by the circumstances of your past, you will attain greater and greater degrees of freedom, which was the promise I made to you as we began this journey.

Now only one thing remains to be done . . .

Ernest Holmes on Spiritual Mind Treatment...

Remember that [Spiritual Mind] Treatment is neither wishing nor willing, it is an affirmation of the presence, the power and the willingness of the Divine Law to specialize Itself for us, to meet every human need.

Can We Talk to God (1934), p. 28.4

Treatment is the process of convincing yourself of the truth of what you say. It is nothing else. When you are self-convinced, then you have set forth into Mind the power that does everything.

Love and Law (2001; teachings 1918-1920), p. 200.2

Treatment is not for the purpose of making things happen; it is to provide, within ourselves, an avenue through which they may happen.

The Science of Mind (1938), p. 274.2

Treatment is not for the purpose of helping us either to avoid reality or to endure unhappy situations. It is for the express purpose of changing situations, and unless situations or conditions are changed as a result of the treatment, we have missed the mark.

Living the Science of Mind (1984), p. 293.4

Living Your Treatment

> *We are what we repeatedly do. Excellence,*
> *then, is not an act, but a habit.*
>
> —ARISTOTLE

In this book I've shared all the information required for the effective use of Spiritual Mind Treatment. This process of affirmative prayer contains all the elements necessary to redirect the power of Universal Mind, thus resulting in the creation of desired conditions, whether those conditions are physically, mentally or emotionally based.

Only one thing can get in the way of the full expression of your treatment and *you* are that one thing. In this final chapter, we will explore ways to make certain you get the most out of your treatments.

What Should I Treat For?

There are so many things going on in each of our lives. How do we choose what to focus on in treatment? This is an important question because there are likely many things we would change about our lives. In response, I offer the following story:

There was once an old and wise chief of a tribe in Africa sitting by his fire admiring the beautiful spring day. Three of the tribe's best young warriors approached their elder and said they wanted to challenge him for the position of tribal chief. He thought for a moment and said that he would accept their challenge if they would accept his.

"What would that challenge be?" they asked.

The chief pointed to a bundle of long sticks that were laying on the ground nearby and said, "Whichever among you can break that bundle of sticks in half, will be named tribal chief, but you each only get one try."

All three agreed.

The first young warrior took the bundle, and holding one end up off the ground, placed his foot in the middle of the bundle and pushed with all his might, but the bundle did not break. The next young warrior took the bundle and set one end up on a rock, and jumped up and down on it, but again the bundle did not break. The third young warrior placed the bundle across the branch of a tree and pulled on both ends, but the bundle did not break.

When they had each had their turn, they returned the bundle to their leader and told him that the task they had been given could not be done. The chief explained that it could be done and took the bundle, untied the binding and proceeded to break each stick in half, one at a time.

Certainly we can change every condition in our lives, however, if we try to tackle all the conditions at once we may become overwhelmed. We have the greatest success when we first determine what is most important and begin there. Even when our lives seem out of control, we can step back and instinctively know which priorities require our most immediate attention. When we handle what is in front of us, we are following the natural course of our lives.

The same wisdom applies when doing Spiritual Mind Treatment. Treat for what is in front of you. Treat for the most important condition you want to change in that moment. Treat knowing that this highest priority is fully manifest in your life right now.

This means that Spiritual Mind Treatment can have many and various applications. Perhaps the most important thing in the moment is that you find your car keys. My wife and I use a little treatment whenever something appears to be misplaced. An example of our treatment might go something like this:

I know that everything exists within the Divine Mind of God, including my car keys. I know they're here now. I claim them, I call them forth, I accept them, and I give thanks for them. And so it is!

We have done this little treatment untold numbers of times and usually before the words are completely spoken; one of us has located the keys. Is it the treatment that finds the keys? No, it's the belief that when we say the treatment, the keys are always found. It is our belief that opens us up to knowing where to find the keys.

Spiritual Mind Treatment is not magic. It is simply a way of directing Universal Mind toward productive outcomes. It is virtually the same process whether we are seeking to find our keys, a parking space near the entrance to the mall, a loving life partner, resolution of a serious health challenge, or any other condition.

Moving Toward vs. Moving Away From

What do you say when looking for your keys or something else misplaced in the moment? I have heard people say repeatedly as they searched for something, "I can't find it!" How would you imagine a hunt for something might go when mixed with such a vehemently opposing affirmation? When we say we can't find something, we are telling our minds not to find it. When we declare that we know where something is, we are telling our minds that we know. What results is that which we declare becomes our reality, and we find whatever was misplaced.

Affirming what you want and turning away from what you don't want applies to all treatment work. When we focus on what we do not want, it may go away some day, but the process of its departure will likely be long and arduous. Moving toward that which we desire is always easier than moving away from that which we do not desire. Even though there may be times when we are very clear about what we don't want, the process of ridding ourselves of any condition will go more quickly and easily when we focus on identifying and claiming the condition that will take its place.

For example, if you are experiencing physical pain caused by an injury, don't attempt to treat for the pain to go away. If you do, your level of pain may actually increase. Instead, know in your treatment that your body is completely healthy, moves easily and functions naturally. By doing this you turn away from the pain, giving it no energy and creating in mind once again your body as healthy and whole. I know many who have used treatment in this way with results that have amazed and confounded their physicians.

Before you begin your treatment, know the precise outcome you desire. The elimination of anything contrary will occur naturally without any effort or attention.

Treatment is Belief Driven

Our individual beliefs systems drive our reality. What we believe, we create. We can do Spiritual Mind Treatment all day long and if we do not believe what we are saying or writing, the conditions we seek to change will not change.

In our spiritual community, we have Practitioners who offer Spiritual Mind Treatment as a gift to friends and members of our community following our Sunday Celebrations of Life. One Sunday, a woman approached one of our Practitioners with a story of some terrible circumstance in her life. They sat together in the sanctuary, discussed the details, and when the Practitioner felt ready, knowing the Truth about this woman, he offered a Spiritual Mind Treatment. When he was done, she thanked him, stood up, took two steps and another person asked her how she was doing. She immediately began to share the same circumstances she had described to the Practitioner. Do you think this woman was open to a change in her circumstance? It would appear not.

The power of treatment dwells in believing what we think, say and do. Treat until you absolutely believe every word. When you absolutely believe your treatment, your demonstration will appear.

Treat Until You See It

One of the most common questions about treatment is, "How many times should we treat about any one condition?" Some who practice Spiritual Mind Treatment say that one treatment is all it takes. For this to be so, there could be no mental encumbrances that would in any way diminish the desired demonstration. If this happens, and it does, that's fantastic!

If however, a treatment does not immediately manifest, consider treating at least once a day until you see an apparent and verifiable manifestation. Treating a condition daily or more often actually constitutes one ongoing treatment, each time building on the consciousness of the last.

By waiting for something to manifest, you may be blocking your treatment. If you catch yourself thinking that your demonstration has not yet shown up, go immediately into treatment, remembering what you know is the Truth. When you absolutely believe that your treatment is true, it will manifest.

Utilizing Practitioners

There will be times and circumstances when anyone may find themselves at a loss as to how to shift a belief and create a desired outcome. They've treated and still feel uncertain, especially because they have not seen any form of demonstration. If and when this happens, there are trained professionals who are willing and able to assist you with your treatment. These people are known either as Licensed Spiritual Practitioners (LSP) or Religious Science Practitioners (RScP).

According to Mary Schroeder and Dr. James Golden in their book, *The Practitioner Handbook*, "A Practitioner is a person who is trained in the art, science and skill of Spiritual Mind Treatment." To be licensed, Practitioners must have completed several years of training, preparing themselves to offer treatment to others. The work of a Practitioner, which is always done with the client's permission, is to realize the Truth and declare into existence a desired condition in the same way we do for ourselves.

If there is a Center for Spiritual Living, a Religious Science Church, Teaching Chapter or Study Group in your community, you can call and ask for a Practitioner referral. Most centers and churches have Practitioners available for prayer support on Sundays following their services. Working with a Practitioner can be a most enlightening and rewarding experience.

Doing Treatments for Others

Offering Spiritual Mind Treatment to another person is something anyone with an understanding of these principles can do. However, there are several important ethical standards that everyone must adhere to in the best interest of the one treating and the one receiving the treatment:

1. Treat only for the one who is directly asking for your assistance. This means you do not treat anyone other than that person, including his or her boss, relatives, friends, or partner.

2. When you treat for another, be certain you have no judgments or emotional sensitivities such as fear or confusion relating to that person or the circumstances surrounding their request. If you do, then you will not be helpful to them.

3. Recognize that what you know in treatment for this person, you also know for yourself. Every treatment you offer to another equally demonstrates in your life because when we treat for anyone, we are always treating for ourselves.

If you desire to use Spiritual Mind Treatment as a spiritual discipline in your life, I encourage you to enroll in classes at your local Centers for Spiritual Living member community. To find a community near you, go to csl.org and click Spiritual Community, then Find a Spiritual Community from the dropdown menu. These classes will offer you a variety of ways to deepen your understanding and use of Spiritual Mind Treatment.

If there is not a community close to you, go to csl.org and click Education and Spiritual Development from the dropdown menu. There you will find an array of online classes where you will learn from the expert teachers and share your experiences with others on their path of awakening.

World Ministry of Prayer

If you wish to receive treatment and cannot contact a Practitioner directly, you may choose to contact Centers for Spiritual Living World Ministry of Prayer online at https://csl.org/world-ministry-of-prayer/. This service has been providing Spiritual Mind Treatment to all who request support since 1937. There is no fee for this service; however, this ministry does accept donations.

Each Licensed Practitioner and minister who participates in offering this service is committed to holding the light of an ever-expanding global consciousness, standing with you in Spiritual Truth and Love. On their website, you can choose to listen to a prerecorded treatment on any of several topics, request that a treatment be offered specifically for you, or you can use "Build a Prayer" as a learning tool for your own personal development in the art of affirmative prayer.

Science of Mind, Guide for Spiritual Living

Another way of expanding your spiritual consciousness is through the semi-monthly publication, *Science of Mind, Guide for Spiritual Living*. In this magazine, which is available online or by mail, you will find interesting articles and columns on spiritual topics and a Daily Guide that gives you quotes from an array of extraordinary teachers and thinkers, including Dr. Ernest Holmes, along with a daily message and affirmation.

To learn more, go to https://scienceofmind.com/ and explore the possibilities.

Spiritual Living Circles

Yet another way to create greater spiritual awareness is to join Spiritual Communities and Spiritual Living Circles from the dropdown menu. There you'll find the information you require to join others in your community who are seeking greater spiritual awareness.

To join an existing circle or start one, go to csl.org and click Spiritual Communities and Spiritual Living Circles from the dropdown menu. There you'll find the information you require to join others in your community who are seeking greater spiritual awareness.

Once you're signed up, you'll start receiving a weekly discussion guide featuring an article from the current edition of *Science of Mind* that contains ideas and questions designed to take you and your circle members into deep and meaningful discussions of a wide variety of spiritual ideas.

Conclusion

Living in a world created, powered and occupied by one dynamic universal force means that we and everything else exist within and as that force. As powerful creative spiritual beings, the greatest power we have dwells in our ability to think our lives into existence. The world we experience around us demonstrates the consciousness that dwells in our minds in the form of thoughts, beliefs, and ideas.

We have within us the ability to change our lives by changing our thinking. Spiritual Mind Treatment offers us a means by which we can accomplish meaningful goals and bring genuine value to our world. When we use Spiritual Mind Treatment as an ongoing spiritual discipline, we live happier, healthier, and fuller lives.

This discipline has worked for thousands of people throughout the world, and it will work for you. I wish you peace and a life filled with blessings as you continue on your journey of discovery. May your prayer always be a knowing of the Truth of Spirit that dwells in you, as you, and all around you.

And so it is.